Stephen & Shirley Channing

A VICTORIAN CYCLIST

~ RAMBLING THROUGH KENT IN 1886 ~

Ôzaru Books

A Victorian Cyclist
by Stephen & Shirley Channing

© Stephen & Shirley Channing, 2011

Published by Ōzaru Books, an imprint of BJ Translations Ltd
Street Acre, Shuart Lane, St Nicholas-at-Wade,
BIRCHINGTON, CT7 0NG, U.K.
www.ozaru.net

First edition published 1 December 2011
Printed by Lightning Source
ISBN: 978-0-9559219-7-1

CONTENTS

4

LIST OF ILLUSTRATIONS

INTRODUCTION

While researching the Keble's Gazette at Margate Library I came across an article entitled 'Rambles Out Of Margate', written in 1886, which appeared to have been written by a cyclist. Not wishing to be distracted from the subject of my research, I decided to copy it to read at a later date. Some months later I rediscovered the article in my 'check it out later' file and it seemed worthy of further investigation. After briefly researching the history of cycling I realised that my accidental discovery offered a very rare insight into the exploits and experiences of a Victorian cyclist.

The anonymous writer not only communicated his passion for cycling but also provided the reader with vast amounts of information on other topics. The text indicated that the writer was well informed on subjects such as history and the local fauna and flora, and that he wanted to share these experiences with others: it seemed a shame that his writings had been consigned to archives, to await a chance discovery.

Cycling was becoming a very popular pastime by the late 1880s and with this in mind I decided to return to the library and carry out further research on the Keble's Gazette, with the aim of establishing if other articles had been written. To my delight I began finding records of other journeys undertaken by our anonymous writer, written both before and after the date of my initial discovery. In all there were descriptions of nine different 'rambles' published in the Gazette over a period of about six months, each covering a different route in East Kent and each starting from the seaside town of Margate. The rambles took the cyclist as far as Faversham and the outskirts of Ashford, varied in distance between 30 miles and 80 miles and in total covered nearly 500 miles of East Kent's less well-known countryside. The longer trips necessitated our cyclist staying overnight at a pub or inn – not forgetting that our cyclist was probably using a tricycle that weighed in at 75 pounds and which pre-dated the invention of pneumatic tyres. Country roads at this time were often rough, tarmac being relatively rare.

Our cyclist appears to have undertaken his rambles between May and August 1886, the first appearing in print in the Keble's Gazette on the 23rd October 1886 and the last on the 9th April 1887. I have been able to find no earlier record of road trips such as these, involving as they do such comprehensive accounts of the experience. These articles offer a wealth of information, not only for the cyclist but for the historian, genealogist and ecologist as well.

The places visited, mainly small hamlets and villages, are seldom mentioned in the tourist books of this period, most likely due to their inaccessibility. Our cyclist, using roads, bridleways, footpaths, woods, the Downs, and even occasionally crossing fields, was determined to reach those places not frequented by the general public. His purpose appears to have been not only to further his personal interest in butterflies and moths, but to bring to the attention of the public the diverse flora and fauna that surrounded them, much of which was indigenous to its locality or apparently rarely found elsewhere in abundance. The intervening decades of demographic expansion and suburbanisation due to social demand have replaced some of the natural habitats of the flora and fauna mentioned by our cyclist over 125 years ago.

Our cyclist recounted many historical facts about places along his routes, often stopping to talk to local individuals about their surroundings or paying a visit to an 'off the beaten track' village or hamlet so as to unravel its history and bring to light past heroes, characters and famous residents. It must be noted that some of the old inscriptions, monuments and brasses in the churches he visited may well have since disappeared, and some of the buildings he spoke of, such as Birchington Hall and several mills, have certainly disappeared, rendering the information provided by our cyclist a potential gold mine for the genealogist or historian.

I have tried to maintain a contemporary feel for the book as far as possible, but it has been necessary to explain some parts of the routes where modern road changes have made it impossible to follow exactly in the Victorian's tracks. In some places parts of the road have been superseded by a major dual carriageway and in others the old roads, and occasionally a whole village, no longer exist. When the original route is interrupted in this way, I have offered an alternative detour. For the most part, however, our Victorian's routes remain pretty well intact.

A contemporary copy of an Ordnance Survey Map for Canterbury & East Kent (Sheet 81 of the David & Charles edition, taken from Sheet 3 (Canterbury), in the Old Series of Ordnance Survey 1 inch maps), has been included in the book, showing the road system as it was in our cyclist's time and thus allowing the journeys he made to be retraced. This map has been divided into 10 numbered sections, which have been enlarged to approximately their original size. The map sections which are needed to follow the routes are indicated at the beginning of each ramble.

Modern directions, including any necessary detours, are given at the end of each individual ramble.

Detailed contemporary and modern maps, highlighting the routes taken, are available to download from www.victoriancyclist.com, and there is no reason why today's cyclist, or hiker, cannot replicate what was achieved by our cyclist in 1886. Many of the journeys can also be largely followed by car.

In order to show the ambivalent attitudes to cycles and cyclists at that time, the chapter 'Cycling in context' offers extracts drawn from the media, with some writers extolling the virtues of the new mode of transport, and others with less positive viewpoints. Conventional attitudes to women's position and role in society are indicated in a separate chapter, as well as within the rambles, the cyclist having a female companion on occasion. Female emancipation and suffrage was still a distant dream at this point in time.

An excerpt is included from Routledge's Boy's Own Annual, dated 1870[1], which indicates the significant improvements made to the design and construction of cycles during our cyclist's lifetime. From this date to the time of his rambles, continuous improvements were being made, as indicated by the media reports of cycling shows, exhibitions, advertisements, etc. Routledge shows the dynamic nature of the industry and the progress being made internationally, with manufacturers from Europe and America vying to outdo each other and produce innovative cycles and accessories.

It appears that the machine used by our Victorian cyclist was a three-wheeler (tricycle), a relatively new contraption of its day. The 'Cripper', pictured below, offers an example of this machine, which was considered to offer a safer and more dignified experience to the rider, particularly to women, than the bicycles of the day. It must be remembered that these tricycles had no gears or pneumatic tyres and were very heavy. The tyres of that particular period were solid Indian Rubber tyres, air-filled pneumatic tyres not being introduced until around 1888. With that in mind, and considering the conditions of the roads at the time, do not scoff at his accomplishments after you have completed the same route on your lighter-than-air, multi-geared aerodynamic model!

From 1881 to 1886 in Great Britain, more tricycles were built than bicycles, even though tricycles were more expensive. It was generally only the upper classes that had the disposable income to buy them and, being perceived as more genteel, they were often purchased for the women in the family. Even the bicycle was very expensive in Victorian England, costing an average worker six months' pay. Enthusiasm for cycling increased considerably in the decade of the 1880s, probably due to advances in technology and design leading to greater safety for the rider.

---

[1] based on a publication from the previous year, "Velocipedes, Bicycles, and Tricycles: How to Make and How to Use them" by 'Velox'

15

Contemporary picture of a tricycle and its rider

I hope that the combination of past and present day information, both in this book and on www.victoriancyclist.com, satisfies the modern reader and offers added interest to what is a unique insight into one of the very earliest modes of mechanical transport, from the Victorian time of experimentation, discovery and innovation.

Stephen Channing

www.victoriancyclist.com

Our Victorian cyclist has left us with a very detailed account of some of our beautiful countryside, giving us a rare insight into East Kent's 'off the beaten track' regions and villages in 1886. Descriptions of social conditions, the rustic nature of the country roads, details of the flora and fauna are all included in his articles, as well as some local history of several of the more secluded hamlets and villages.

Some of the information given by our Victorian cyclist may be of more interest to some than to others and, in order to preserve the contemporary feel and the flow of the narrative in the book, a website has been created, www.victoriancyclist.com, which holds further information about the many and various topics shared by our narrator. Also, while the book includes sections of the type of map that our author would have used in 1886, showing quite clearly the country roads that existed during our cyclist's time, these are also included in www.victoriancyclist.com, with the routes highlighted, in order that they can be easily downloaded and printed for ease of use.

There are various companies today that provide copies of old Ordnance Survey Maps but, for those who would like to attempt a ramble that our Victorian cyclist accomplished in 1886 without any of our modern day aids, the maps illustrated in the book are of the type he used. Remember, though, that although remarkably little has changed in the remote countryside in which our cyclist rambled, there are now a few dead-ends created by modern-day dual carriageways ripping through our beautiful countryside – not unlike the Roman roads did hundreds of years before. If the reader would prefer to trace the route on a modern map, a visit to www.victoriancyclist.com will allow the downloading of the required section in an up to date format, with the route highlighted.

www.victoriancyclist.com provides details of modern day services along our cyclist's routes, including shops and hostelries from which today's traveller can obtain refreshments or a room, among other things. Many of these establishments were patronised by our Victorian cyclist.

www.victoriancyclist.com includes photographs and modern day information about some of the villages to which our cyclist referred, alongside some local history, in order that those interested may compare the villages of today to those visited in 1886.

Readers interested in the fauna and flora identifed by our cyclist will also find more details on www.victoriancyclist.com. Pictures of all the fauna and flora to which he referred are included, for those who may be interested in attempting to rediscover them in their Victorian habitats.

The website www.victoriancyclist.com will provide all the necessary information for modern day cyclists to follow the Victorian rambles. It will also expand on many of the topics to which our cyclist referred.

As our cyclist would say – En Avant!

Acknowledgements

Thanks to Margate Library staff for facilitating access to the material that led to the production of this book.

Thanks to Terry and Jenny Fearn, from Thanet Road Club, for taking on some of the rambles and providing valuable feedback.

Special thanks to Steve's brother Malcolm for his valuable time spent designing, producing and maintaining the website: www.victoriancyclist.com

Above all, thanks to my wife Shirley for working with me on this book and for getting the text into shape: this was definitely a two-person production!

THE RAMBLES OF A VICTORIAN CYCLIST

1886

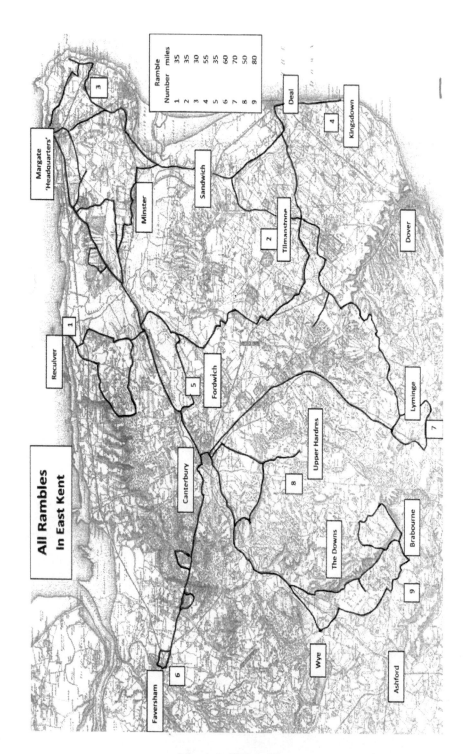

Ramble Number	miles
1	35
2	35
3	30
4	55
5	35
6	60
7	70
8	50
9	80

All Rambles In East Kent

Map of all Rambles

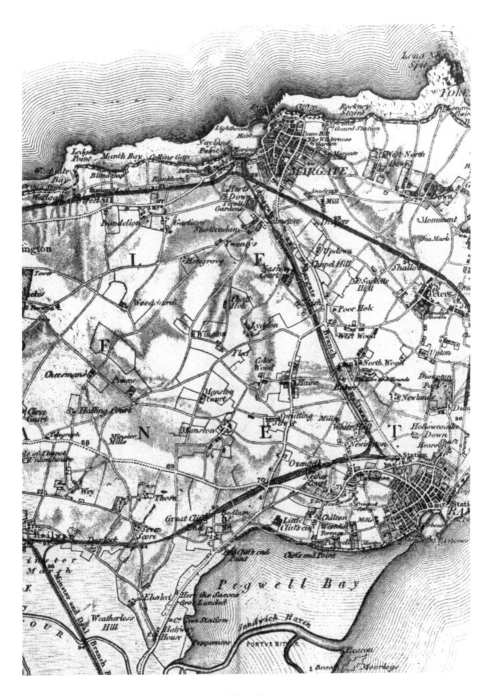

Map 1

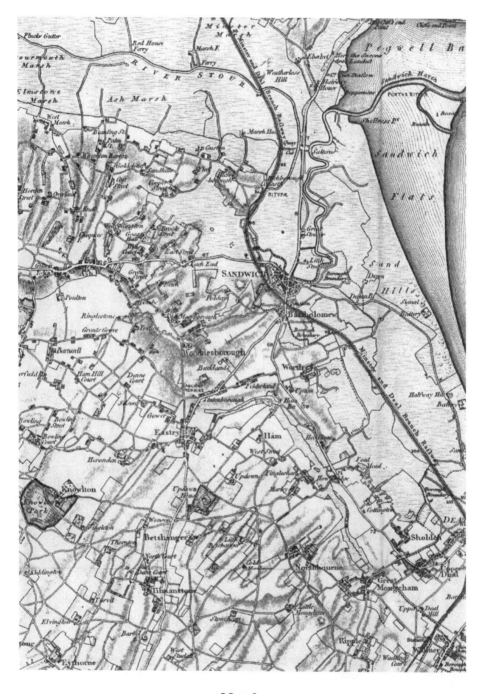

Map 2

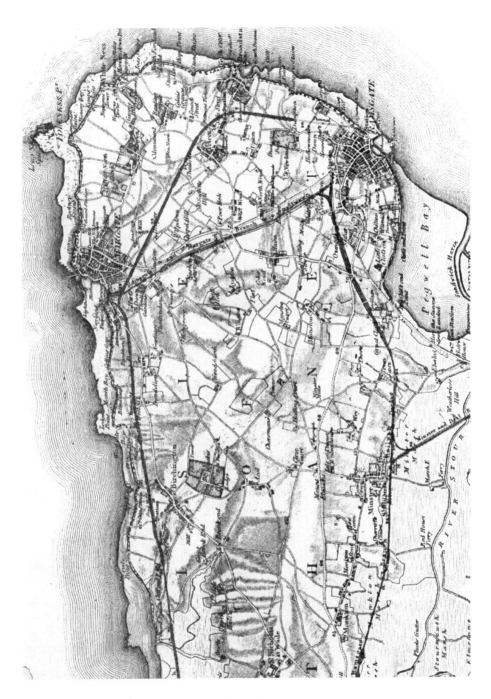

Map 3

Map 4

Map 5

25

Map 6

Map 7

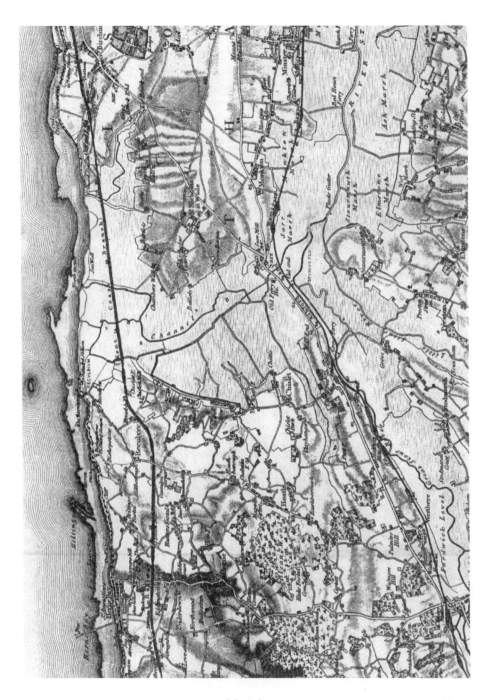

Map 8

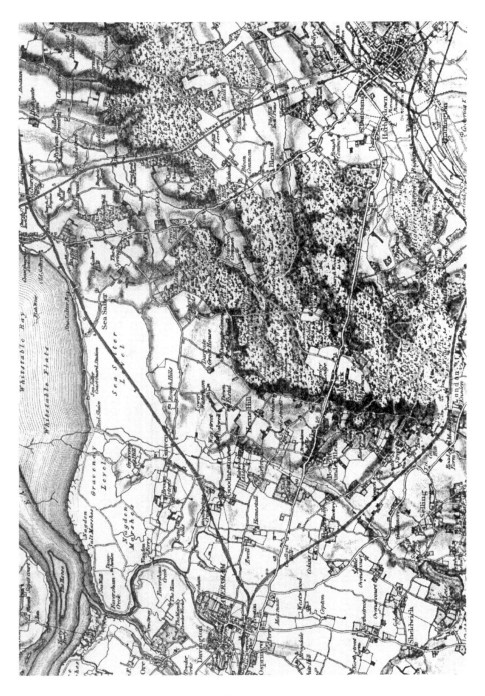

Map 9

Map 10

RAMBLE 1

(Maps 3, 8)

Approximately 35 miles

Margate

Birchington

Hale

St Nicholas-at-Wade

Sarre

Upstreet

Hoath

East Blean Wood

West Blean Wood

Herne

Reculvers

Hillborough

Marsh Row

Chislet

Upstreet

Sarre

St Nicholas-at-Wade

Birchington

Margate

Marine Parade circa 1900

Margate 1889

To the Editor of the 'Keble's Gazette'

Sir – The cyclist possessed of a good machine, starting from the head quarters in Margate for a day's run in the country, has a most interesting district before him, and one in every way suitable for pleasant rambles. The roads are generally good and, though the country is undulating, there are few hills so steep as to make a dismounting necessary. Moreover, every village, hamlet, farmhouse, and I had almost said every cottage, possesses a history of its own or contains some novelty which helps to make such rambles delightful. With your kind permission I will give in a chatty manner a description of one or two rambles. I presume Mr Editor, that both you and your readers are interested in trifles as well as in more important issues and I feel convinced that you will pardon me at times becoming excited over the beauties of an old ruin, a gabled roof, a way-side flower, or a gilded butterfly.

When starting this ramble one needs to travel up Margate's High Street from the harbour area. Parts of the High Street have been pedestrianised during certain times of the day, necessitating a dismount. On reaching St John's Church, at the end of the High Street, keep to the right of the church and enter the one-way system (A255) for about 100m until you reach some crossroads. Bear right onto the Ramsgate Road (A254), under the railway bridge (once the site of East Margate Station) and on to the traffic lights. Turn right at the traffic lights into College Road (A2052 – known in our cyclist's time as Salmeston Rise). To visit Salmestone Grange turn left at the next set of traffic lights, into Nash Road. The Grange is about 100m on the right. Otherwise, go straight across these traffic lights into Shottendane Road.

Margate High Street

Margate High Street

But to begin my day's ramble, my iron steed is ready having been cleaned and oiled and lamps fixed. I mount and make my way slowly up the High street. As I pass by St John's Church, being in a contemplative frame of mind, I try to calculate how many generations have worshipped in that grand old church; I wonder too, what was the state of society in Margate when locks and keys, such as may be seen in the vestry, and which are certainly not of the Willenhall Pattern, were in use, and what was the standard of morality when a coffin maker appropriated a beautiful old brass (one of a number in the church) and used the reverse side for a coffin plate. I also wonder what was the state of education when our forefathers spelt the name of the mother of us all 'Heva[2]' (see old black leather bible).

St John's Church

---

[2]In the Old Testament, Eve is called Heva.

34

During these cogitations I have passed East Margate Railway Station, have turned out of the main Ramsgate road and have reached Salmestone Grange.

Salmestone Grange in 1865

The remains of some monastic buildings, used for farm purposes, attract my attention and at the same moment the cross face of the tenant farmer appears on the scene. I was almost tempted to request his permission to see the inside of his barn, but second thoughts are best trusted, is my motto. Shottendane is the next farmhouse approached, and here a feeling of envy comes over me as I think that by no stratagem can we induce even one nightingale to pay our garden a visit and greet us with its melody, while it is on record that this songster was so plentiful here last spring as to become a nuisance. Hengrove with its grove of trees is soon reached; the lichen thereon provides food for a tiny moth not to be found everywhere, and specimens of the indigo settle on the trunks in early summers.

Hengrove

Now I have a decent hill to mount, with a flowery bank on one side of the road supporting a few stunted blackthorn bushes. On these bushes the winter nests of the brown tail moth may be seen, but don't touch them, or the pretty larvae either, for the hairs emit a poisonous ingredient which is very irritating to the hands, face, and neck.

The signpost at the top of the hill shows that Garlinge may be reached on my right, where the ancient gateway of 'Dent de Lyon', may be seen, but I head for Quex Park.

Dent de Lyon

Arriving at the lodge gates, I am within a short distance of Woodchurch Farm and I take the opportunity to pay it a hurried visit. The farmhouse may be taken as a fair example of farmhouses in Thanet, where frequently thirsty and tired cyclists may obtain most welcome refreshments. On the opposite side of the road is situated the kitchen garden and a labouring man is busily engaged planting vegetables upon the site of the old church: nothing remains but the foundations.

Woodchurch Farm

I return to Quex, on my left hand the park and on my right a magnificent hop garden – passing along the perfection of a country road. The hop garden ends, and the view takes in Westgate-on-Sea and the vast ocean on the right, Birchington Hall ensconced amidst trees in front and glimpses of the Waterloo Tower in the park.

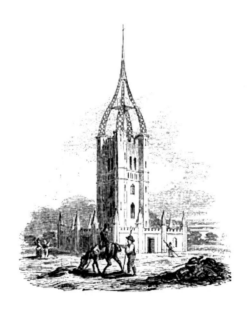

The Waterloo Tower

Birchington Hall, as it looked in 1886
Latterly the site of Spurgeon's Homes, the Hall has now been demolished and replaced by a new housing estate.

Unfortunately the unevenness of the roadway prevents my enjoyment of the view and all my attention is required for the management of my machine. I enter the village of Birchington close by the Hall and unconsciously pass over some extensive caves which extend under the roadway; they are said to have been used by smugglers, but they are more probably illegal lime pits.

The road described above (Park Road) continues past Quex Park, past modern houses on either side of the road and across a small roundabout. The road has been blocked to vehicles at this junction with the Canterbury Road, where our cyclist 'enter(s) the village close by the Hall'. However, pedestrians and cyclists can still access the Canterbury Road here. Turn left, and then continue on to Birchington Square.

At the present time Birchington is a highly respectable village, with a reputation for being determined to make its way in the world with the aid of its 'Bay' and its 'Bungalows'; but the oldest inhabitants are supposed to have, most of them, been engaged more or less in smuggling transactions, a favourite 'hide' for 'tubs' being under the roof, to which ascent was gained by steps fixed inside the chimney. A chimney wide enough for this purpose may at present be seen attached to the outside of a cottage in Birchington Street.

Leaving my steed at the Powell Arms, near the entrance to the churchyard, I pay a visit to the grave of the artist poet, Dante Gabriel Rossetti, which is situated within a few feet of the church porch.

Gabriel Dante Rossetti (1828-82)

Rossetti's grave
Designed by Rossetti's friend and fellow painter, Ford Maddox Brown, and erected by Rossetti's family in 1882.

Birchington Church and the Powell Arms in the background, circa 1900

I next enter the beautiful old church, and an ancient font attracts my attention. Immediately above the font is the 'Rossetti' window, a work of art which alone will repay a journey from Margate.

The *tout ensemble* of the church denotes loving care on the part of its custodians. Amongst the objects of interest therein may be mentioned the modern and florid reredos, the effigies on the tomb of Sir Henry Crispe in the Crispe Chapel, various brasses in a fair state of preservation, the latter probably owing their safety to the zeal of some Protestant in anti Papist times carefully cutting away from each description 'Pray for the soul of ...'

Brass in Birchington Church
Notice the cut away section of the writing of this brass – the Latin words for 'Pray for the soul of' have been removed.

Archaeologists will be interested in noting the nave and two aisles under one roof, the lower at the east end, and a lancet window in a peculiar position in the

40

Crispe Chapel. The lid of the old parish chest is carefully deposited between a pew and the west end of the church, and the old font cover may be seen stored away in the belfry.

Old cottages at Brooksend

En Avant! An easy run out of Birchington takes me into the hedgeless Thanet fields once more, into a district much frequented by the Thanet Harriers [fox hunters]. I proceed down Brooks End hill with brakes on, and at the bottom one of those events happens to me which probably happens only to cyclists gliding silently along the highway on Indian-rubber wheels. Who but a cyclist has come close to a hen partridge with her tiny but active chicks, and passed by without disturbing them. Who but a cyclist has seen in the dusk of an early spring evening a couple of hares within a few feet of the road racing about in such a manner as to prove the truth of the old adage, 'Mad as a March hare!' and after watching them for some time, has left them to their wonderful gyrations?

Brooksend

41

Well, at the foot of Brooks End hill, a scream causes brake to be tightened and I find myself the centre of a group comprising a hare and two dogs. The screams proceed from the hare which, in its endeavours to escape from the pursuing dogs, has run straight into one of the big wheels of my machine, and the force of the concussion causes it to turn a complete somersault whilst the two dogs stop in their pursuit and look on in mute amazement. The hare coolly creeps under the machine, looks round, takes in the situation and then darts off into a drain close by before the dogs recover from their surprise. Ascending another hill I get within sight of St Nicholas Church. Here in the early spring, a turning on the right, half way between Brooks End and St Nicholas heading to Hale farm, is a notable place for violets of all shades of colour from white to dark violet. If anyone desires to know my ideal of a picturesque farmhouse let him visit Hale when the chestnuts, hawthorns and orchard trees are in blossom, or when the winter roses are in bloom in January. This too, is a noted spot for *danainae* (*Danaus Plexippus* or Monarch butterfly). I, however, pass along on the dusty road from whence no idea whatsoever can be obtained of the lovely paddocks situated within such a short distance.

Hale Farm

Hale Farm and its surroundings offer today's cyclist an attractive detour, and one may wish to utilise this alternative route to St Nicholas-at-Wade, rather than continuing on the modern dual carriageway:

42

When leaving Brooks End and entering onto the dual carriageway, continue for about half a mile, until reaching a turning on the right with an old plough share at its entrance. This is Netherhale Farm road and has a sign saying that it is a dead-end. It is a dead-end for motorised traffic but not for pedestrians, horses or bikes. When you reach the end of this road turn left, onto a track which takes you to Shuart Farm. On reaching Shuart Farm bear left onto Shuart Lane. This leads to a 'T' junction that has a large foot bridge opposite. Shuart Lane has now been bisected by the A299 Thanet Way. Continue across the large foot bridge and along Shuart Lane into the middle of the village of St Nicholas-at-Wade.

As I approach St Nicholas (known as St Nicholas at Wade) I get a grand view. On my right the twin towers of Reculvers and the ocean, in front the woods of Blean and the valley of the Stour and on my left across the Stour valley the North Downs, extending almost to Dover. St Nicholas is a village which has seen better days. The church is an immense structure for the number of inhabitants and will well repay a visit as it contains numerous objects and monuments of interest.

St Nicholas-at-Wade with its church in the background

The capitals to the pillars are especially fine. The tower reminds one of those at Herne, St Peter's Thanet, Chatham, Rainham, Boughton-Under-Blean and many others which were lovingly restored about the same period. The view from the top of the tower is magnificent, with old dilapidated cottages and large farmhouses which give a character to the village of its own, and as I return to the high road, I hope that the Christmas of 1886 may be more prosperous than that of 1885 when on Christmas Day a notice was posted on the door to the effect that the Vicar and Churchwardens were destitute of all funds for distribution amongst the poor.

The Bell Inn, St Nicholas-at-Wade, circa 1900

A few minutes hard riding brings me to the Ville of Sarre and I alight at the touring house[3]. Sarre has a wonderful history of its own; hundreds of our Saxon forefathers lay undisturbed close to the windmill until a thirst for knowledge on the part of the public caused their graves to be opened some years ago.

The Crown Inn
The 'touring house' mentioned above is often referred to as the Cherry Brandy House.

---

[3] A 'cyclist-friendly' establishment, approved by the Cyclists' Touring Club

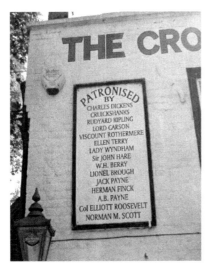

Plaques on the wall of the Crown Inn

These bear testament to famous people who have patronised the establishment.

Sarre Mill

This photograph shows the Mill as our cyclist may have seen it. The site occupied by the Mill is surrounded by ancient Anglo-Saxon graves.

The list of articles found in the graves is a touching one. The warrior was buried with his sword and other weapons, the lady with her beads and trinkets, a little child with its toys and the tradesman with his materials. Sarre cemetery has the honour of having produced more swords in proportion to graves than any other similar burial ground in this county, testifying to the wealth of the former inhabitants of this village.

Tradition says there were formerly three churches here, but all have disappeared and the only place of worship is a tiny Wesleyan Chapel.

The Wesleyan Chapel
This is now a private residence.

During my gossip with the landlord of the touring house, who is intimately acquainted with the Mansion House once occupied by Queen Elizabeth, I try the gravity of his ale and his 'Sarre' cakes or sip his excellent cherry brandy, but carefully eschew politics.

Mansion House
This elegant building, directly opposite the Crown Inn, has replaced the Mansion House, once occupied by Queen Elizabeth I.

46

On these rambles the rider requires more frequent 'oiling' than his machine and after such occasional oilings the machine moves more freely. I now run along Sarre Wall, as a mile and a half of the road is called. This wall is dead level and almost straight across what was once the estuary of the Wantsum, where Roman galleys have sailed on their journey to London. A row of poplar trees and a ditch are on each side of the road, which has its history. Formerly the road wound its way across the marshes in a very devious manner. Contracts were invited for a new road to be made in a straight line. One contractor's estimate, which was accepted, was so ridiculously low in contrast with the others, that everybody prophesised his failure. In effect he simply dug out a ditch, thereby raising a bank and constructed his roadway on top, realising a handsome profit. I am now outside the Isle of Thanet, and, with bated breath, I confess that the flora outside at once shows improvement, though an assiduous person has been able to obtain nearly 300 wild flowers in Thanet within the short space of three weeks. As I ascend the hill towards Upstreet, I become aware that hedges are growing on each side of me, and soon I am able to search for flowers in woods and copses, instead of being obliged to confine myself, as in Thanet, to a narrow strip of uncultivated ground upon the top of a receding cliff.

At Upstreet I turn to the right and descend a short but very steep hill, requiring all my brake power, into the valley of the little 'Blean' river – a most interesting spot for botanists.

At the top of the next hill I take the road pointed out by the signpost as leading to Hoath, and pass an interesting old farmhouse with the date (17th century) to be read very plainly.

The 'interesting old farmhouse'
The present owners confirmed that the 17th century date mentioned has long since disappeared and that parts of the building actually date back to the 13th century. High hedgerows now obscure the farmhouse from the road.

I might stop at Hoath, but my ramble will be shorn of several very interesting features. To my gratification I notice that the door of the small church stands open and I am able to enter without having to get the keys at the vicarage. A broken holy water stoup in the porch prepares me somewhat for the ancient interior, which has been most carefully restored. The building is in such an admirable condition that a casual observer might think the church a modern erection, but the archaeologist recognises at a glance the Norman walls, pillars and arches. The chancel is in keeping with the rest of the church, and two or three brasses tell of the wealthy families who resided here 400 years ago.

Hoath Church
The holy water stoup in the porch appears to have been restored since our cyclist visited in 1886.

Prince of Wales pub, Hoath, circa 1885

The Gate Inn near Hoath, circa 1900

Hoath Mill, circa 1900

From Hoath a good road runs through East Blean Wood, and I am soon in the centre of the wood with low undergrowth and tall oak trees on each side. I place my machine under the shadow of a gigantic stack of faggots and walk about some open spaces watching the flight of the Pearl-Bordered Fritillary *(Argynnis Euphrosune)* as it flits about in plenty in the sunshine.

I satisfy myself that there is only one species of fritillary here and, as my destination is West Blean Wood, I presently continue my journey and arrive at the

49

Fox and Hounds, near Blean. This comfortable inn I make my headquarters for the day.

The Fox and Hounds
This is now a private residence.

Blean windmill

The village of Blean

Now I am on the edge of one of the largest woods in Kent, for it extends under different names and with here and there a few cultivated fields, some 12 or 15 miles as far as Mad Thom's Oak[4], and the hills above Boughton. Today I confine myself to a very small portion of the wood, since my object is to find, if possible, a few specimens of the Wood Fritillary *(Melitea Athalia)*. After a careful search I succeed in getting four very good specimens. On being caught in the net each specimen drew in its legs and feigned death, but I know from former experience that they are able to recover their activity and escape if not sharply watched.

Other insects fell to lot during my search for the above, such as the Duke of Burgundy Fritillary *(N. Lucina),* the Green Hair Streak *(Thecla Rubi),* Cream Spot Tiger Moth *(Arctia Villica),* and the tiny but striking *Octomaculata,* &c. &c. When just about to leave the wood, I notice the approach of the keeper. According to my usual custom, I enter into a friendly conversation with him and find the truth of the remark once made to me, 'A little oil is better than a pint of vinegar'. In the course of conversation, I discover that we are old acquaintances, having met before in the New Forest.

As the sun begins to sink towards the west, I return to my headquarters, and after a wash and brush up and a substantial meal (most important items in a day's ramble), start homeward. Having an hour or so to spare, I decide to return to Upstreet by a different route. I quietly pass through Blean and skirt Strode Park into the village of Herne. I look in at the church, rendered memorable by having had Bishop Ridley as one of its rectors, and make a note of font, reredos and half a dozen large brasses for future investigation.

---

[4] See Ramble 6

Herne Church

Bishop Ridley
Ridley became vicar of Herne in 1538.

I then ride steadily on until I reach Reculvers.

Follow the A291 through the village of Herne and turn right at the little roundabout into School Lane, which eventually becomes Broomfield Road. On reaching the end of Broomfield Road, continue straight over a rather messy junction, past Ford Road on the right, to the 'T' junction. Turn right into Margate Road, and continue to a 'T' junction at Hawthorn. Turn left at the junction into Heart In Hand Road, which crosses over the dual carriageway (Thanet Way) and heads towards Hillborough. Heart In Hand Road eventually becomes Sweechbridge Road. On leaving Hillborough bear right into Reculver Lane, past St Mary the Virgin Church and on to Reculver Towers.

Here I simply make notes, for time will not allow of a hunt of fossils under that geologist's Elysium, the Bishopstone cliff, nor a walk round King Ethelbert's castle wall, with a visit to the top of the twin towers, and an inspection of the ruins, including the apse of the old Roman church.

The twin towers of Reculver
For hundreds of years the twin towers of the 12th century church at Reculver have aided ships to navigate the treacherous waters of the English Channel. The houses to the right of the towers no longer exist but the King Ethelbert Inn, on the right in the foreground, is a thriving pub today.

On leaving Reculvers I put spurs (metaphorically) to my steed, pass Hillborough and Marsh Row, and reach Chislet, close by the ancient church.

When leaving Reculver follow the same route used by our cyclist, that is, take the first road on the left signposted for Chislet, called Brook Lane. A modern dual carriageway now crosses this old road, but a short diversion will enable the modern cyclist to continue to Chislet:

53

About a mile along Brook Lane, take the first turning on the right, signposted to Marshside. This road crosses the dual carriageway (A299, Thanet Way) before arriving at a 'T' junction. Turn left at this junction and follow the road through Marshside. At the next 'T' junction, turn left onto Church Lane, and head towards Chislet.

An immense number of house martens attract my attention; indeed, I count as many as forty-nine nests under the eaves of one house.

In the church a service is proceeding and I quietly enter during the hymn before the sermon. After the service I make time to examine the objects of interest, the large chancel, the site of the priest's room, the curious and immense square pillars and, last but not least, the well preserved Norman doorway leading to the tower. As I leave the church I feel regret that any of its beauty should be marred by such an unsightly wall colour.

19th century painting of Chislet Church

I remount, and the vicar and his curate give me a friendly nod of recognition as I pass them on the road. But *tempus fugit*, and now I must hasten on, or I shall be benighted. I must emulate the speed of 'Smuggler Bill', of Ingoldsby fame:

"Down Chislet lane, so free and so fleet,
Rides Smuggler Bill, and away to Upstreet,
Sarre Bridge is won"

Out of Chislet, continue straight over the crossroads and then follow the road round two sharp bends, into Sandpit Hill followed by Nethergong Hill. Turn left at the 'T' junction, onto the major A28 Island Road to Margate.

At Sarre the shadows are falling fast, but I hesitate to light up, and have my reward in the weird forms which present themselves to my view as I ascend the hill towards St Nicholas.

Lights now begin to shine brightly on sea and land as the darkness deepens. Before entering Birchington I light my lamps, and then ride into Margate without a stoppage. I retire to rest and sleep soundly feeling, like the village blacksmith, that:

> *"Something attempted, something done,*
> *Has earned a night's repose[5]"*

---

[5] Henry Wadsworth Longfellow, The Village Blacksmith

Modern directions for Ramble 1

From Margate's Turner Contemporary Art Gallery:

When starting this ramble one needs to travel up Margate's High Street from the harbour area. Parts of the High Street have been pedestrianised during certain times of the day, necessitating a dismount. On reaching St John's Church, at the end of the High Street, keep to the right of the church and enter the one-way system (A255) for about 100m to some crossroads. Bear right onto the Ramsgate Rd (A254, under the railway bridge (once the site of East Margate Station) and on to the traffic lights

Turn right at traffic lights into College Rd

At the next set of traffic lights either turn left to visit Salmestone Grange or continue across the traffic lights into Shottendane Rd

In approximately 2 ½ miles there are some crossroads

To visit Woodchurch turn left into Park Rd, alternatively, turn right into Park Rd and continue to a small roundabout

Take the second exit into what appears to be a dead end, but there is access into Canterbury Rd for cyclists and pedestrians only

Turn left onto Canterbury Rd and continue to the roundabout in Birchington Square. Take the first exit and continue along Canterbury Rd

At the next roundabout, take second exit

Take the first road on the right into The Length, for St Nicholas-at-Wade

After visiting St Nicholas-at-Wade return to Canterbury Rd and turn right

At the small roundabout in Sarre take the second exit onto Island Rd (A28)

At Upstreet, turn right into Nethergong Hill, towards Chislet

Take the first left into Marley Rd, and continue to Hoath

At Hoath turn left at the 'T' junction into Church Rd and continue to a staggered junction. Turn left then right into Hicks Forstal Rd

Follow Hicks Forstal Rd for 2 miles and turn right at the 'T' junction onto the Canterbury Rd (A291)

Continue along Canterbury Rd for 2 miles into Herne

At the small roundabout in Herne take the second exit into School Lane

After ½ mile School Lane becomes Broomfield Rd

Continue along Broomfield Rd for 2 miles to a messy junction

Continue straight across this messy junction to a 'T' junction and turn right into Margate Rd

At the next 'T' junction turn left into Heart in Hand Rd

At the next 'T' junction at Hillborough, turn right into Reculver Lane, passing St Mary's Church on the right, and arrive at the ruins of Reculver Towers

Return along Reculver Lane until reaching a turning on the left called Brook Lane, signposted to Chislet

Continue along Brook Lane for 1 mile until reaching a turning on the right signposted for Chislet. This traverses the Thanet Way (A299)

Turn left at the 'T' junction and follow the road for 2 miles to Marshside

Turn left at the 'T' junction into Church Lane, and continue for 1 mile to Chislet

From Chislet continue for 2 miles towards Upstreet to a 'T' junction

Turn left onto the A28 Island Rd towards Margate

Continue following the directions for Margate and then the directions for the Turner Contemporary

RAMBLE 2

(Maps 1, 2)

Distance approximately 35 miles

Margate

Sandwich

Ham Ponds

Statenborough

Eastry

Tilmanstone

Sandwich

Ebbsfleet

Sevenscore

Cliffsend

Margate

Margate

This ramble must of necessity be a short one, for as I pass St John's Church at starting the clock strikes the hour of one in the afternoon. It is early in June, and the day is most suitable for a cyclist, being bright and sunny but not too hot, for a gentle breeze from the south east cools the air. My destination is fixed, and I prepare for a sharp spin, the problem for immediate solution being the length of time the journey will occupy.

Margate Jetty, circa 1900

The first milestone on the road to Ramsgate is soon reached, and here I dismount and stow away all surplus wraps. This done to my satisfaction, I resume my ride (1.05 pm), ascend Chapel Hill, and reach the second milestone in 5½ minutes, not bad time considering the hill. At the old turnpike gate I take the road for Sandwich and Deal, and pass through Haine, three miles from Margate (1.15 pm). The road is in almost perfect condition, and at 1.20 pm I have passed both the two milestones, situated quarter of a mile distant from each other, representing four miles from Margate. 5th mile (1.24 pm) – down the hill to the 'Sportsman', and along the level to the 6th mile (1.29 pm) at the coastguard station; 7th mile – Stonar Cut (1.34 pm), and here a perfectly level road makes me quicken my pace, for the pleasure of riding at full speed on a good road is not always obtainable, and I complete the 8th mile in a few seconds less than four minutes.

I enter Sandwich under the 'Barbican' (1.43 pm), go straight ahead, get well jolted as I rush over the pavement, and again at the level crossing at the railway.

The Barbican, Sandwich

To negotiate the modern one-way system, turn left and around the Barbican into the High St. Follow the one-way system to a 'T' junction. Turn left into New St and follow this road over the level crossing to a roundabout. Take the first exit onto the Deal Rd.

At the fork I take the Deal road, and now I have not much further to go. Less than a mile along the Deal road a turning to the left leads to Worth (provincially pronounced and spelt Word), another turning on the right goes to a windmill and to the little village of Ham; I take the latter road, pass close by the windmill and some cottages, descend into a valley, and dismount when I arrive at a little stream in the vicinity of Ham Ponds (1.55).

Ham Windmill
The windmill itself no longer exists but buildings associated with it have survived.

Ham Ponds

The little stream at Ham

It has been said that exercise is beneficial for everybody, also that the pursuit of butterflies causes people to take exercise – *ergo* the pursuit of butterflies is beneficial. This is putting the value of entomology on a very low basis, yet I am not ashamed to own that I owe this day's most agreeable ride to a desire to see one of our local butterflies in its native haunts. So local is the species *Melitea Artemis* (in English, the Greasy Fritillary) that not one of my friends could tell me where to find it, and as I open a gate and push my machine into a field for greater safety I console myself with the thought that if unsuccessful in my pursuit today I cannot fail to have a pleasant ramble today. The little stream is here kept clear of weeds, and I have not walked many yards along the bank before a specimen of *Artemis*, recognised at once, crosses my path, and I derive immense satisfaction from an examination of its beautiful markings and place it in my collecting box. In about half an hour I have obtained five specimens, and, knowing that the insect is gregarious in its habits, I decide I am not in the 'metropolis'. The stream being too wide for me to get across without the aid of a leaping pole, as used in the fens, I return to the gate at the road, and there cross to the opposite bank, where I find the Fritillary in plenty, flying about three or four together, and I capture about a score specimens, in order to pick out from them a good series.

After my successful operations I commence 'prospecting'. The district is new to me; probably the whole valley is a swamp in the winter. Now it is covered in rich vegetation, a perfect El Dorado for the botanist. Here and there are enclosures containing clumps of willow, alder, and other shrubs, desirable spots for the ornithologist. In the more open spaces of these enclosures are faded

63

remnants of the spring flowers, primroses and hyacinths, while as yet the summer flowers have not fully bloomed. I am surrounded by so many interesting natural objects that the time flies unconsciously by, until I suddenly discover it is four o'clock, when I decide to proceed to Eastry for refreshment.

By the advice of a resident I return past the windmill to the Deal road, and from thence get a good road, via Statenborough, to Eastry, which is a flourishing village set on a hill.

On leaving Ham Ponds, return to the main Deal road and turn left then left again, into Felderland Lane which, as our cyclist mentions, will take you 'via Statenborough to Eastry.

At the bottom of the hill is a pond covered with water lilies. The church is conspicuous with a tower similar to that of St Nicholas (previously described), its west face being worthy of notice; the nave also is peculiar, and from its height and narrowness resembles an inverted ship. There are, too, some curious fresco paintings over the chancel arch, and in various parts of the church may be seen holy water stoups, more than one piscina, and other remnants of the pre-Reformation period. Brasses to the memory of the 'Nevinsons', with a helmet belonging to the same family, and a monument to Captain Harvey, interest me as I look round the church; and a curious circle on one of the pillars, supposed to contain a table for finding the 'Sunday Letter', is pointed out to me. Antiquaries will discover that the history of Eastry dates back to a very early period.

Eastry Church

The High Street, Eastry

The Cross, Eastry

I next proceed down the hill on the road to Dover, and at the bottom of the hill note a pond similar to that passed before reaching Eastry, and opposite to the pond the cultivated rock-rose *(helianthemum)* is seen in great profusion.

A new dual carriageway (A256 Dover Road) has been built to replace the old road. On leaving Eastry continue down Lower Street for about 500m, when the

65

road becomes the old Dover road. At the approach to the modern roundabout, there is a cycle path (number 15) on the right. This cycle path is the old Dover road, running alongside the new dual carriageway. It periodically joins the old Dover road and eventually reaches Tilmanstone.

The road now becomes chalky, and along its left side runs a bank 'whereon the wild Thyme grows', a famous place for butterflies. There is a continuous rise to Betshanger, the seat of Lord Northbourne, which I pass on the left. I stop at a plantation of small fir trees, and enter into a conversation with a labourer, who gives me a pleasant account of Betshanger, and, amongst other interesting details, tells me of two wonderful yew trees which meet in the churchyard, one having been planted by Mr Gladstone and the other by a famous general (Viscount Hardinge).

The village of Tilmanstone lies on the right hand, at a short distance from Betshanger, and a few minutes' ride brings me to the church, a small structure on the slope of a hill, very prettily situated. The lych-gate and church door are open, and I find that the interior consists of chancel and nave, there being seats in it for about 80 persons. It has undergone restoration very recently, and a peculiar appearance is given by the use of white pine for the pews and roof instead of the more customary brown stained wood. The north wall of the nave is evidently the most ancient portion of the church, but all parts are interesting. There are traces of Norman work, transition, and Early English. In the chancel is a mural brass worthy of special notice, since it is the latest monument erected to the family of the name of 'Fogge', which at one time possessed great wealth and immense influence in various parts of East Kent, and which sank to poverty and oblivion. It is said that the last lineal descendent of this once powerful family married a shepherd at Eastry in the last century, and here its history ceases. While I am looking round the church, a lady connected to it enters, and supplies me with much interesting information concerning the neighbourhood and the restoration of the church. I learn from her of an ancient deserted village at hand, where the foundations of houses can be traced in the fields; also of various relics kept at the rectory. My informant speaks regretfully of an oversight the workmen made at the restoration of the church, "they left no place for the owls that formerly roosted in the roof." With this feeling of regret I cordially agree, having a great affection for the owl. Whenever I pass by a country church at dusk I recollect:

> *"That from yonder ivy-mantled tower,*
> *The moping owl does to the moon complain*
> *Of such as wandering near her secret bower,*
> *Molest her ancient solitary reign.[6]"*

---

[6] Thomas Grey, Elegy written in a country churchyard

Tilmanstone Church

The old stocks at Tilmanstone Church

Star Inn, Tilmanstone, circa 1880

The hand pump at Sandwich

From Tilmanstone I start homewards. I ride leisurely along the road through Eastry. Approaching Sandwich I notice the chapel of St Bartholomew's Hospital, used like that at Salmestone for a barn. A stream similar to that in the Ham valley flows by the side of the road into Sandwich, and supplies the town with water, no uncommon sight being a pump in one of the chief streets showing the whereabouts of this stream. I leave my machine at the Sandwich Arms, and find Sandwich one of the most interesting towns I have visited. Old-fashioned houses with overhanging storeys give quite a Flemish character to the town, but signs are not wanting to show that its prosperity is a thing of the past. I walk along the city wall, now a pleasant promenade, and at St Clement's Church stop to admire the beautiful Norman tower, and its well-restored interior. On the wall of the churchyard grows in profusion the 'pellitory of the wall', a plant only attached to old walls. Here it is in such plenty that I am not surprised to learn from a resident that for many years it has supplied a local herbalist with the chief ingredient of his noted ointment.

The Sandwich Arms
This is now a private residence.

Following the city wall I trace the site of the ancient castle, examine the only city gate left standing [Fisher Gate], and then walk leisurely to St Mary's Church, which I find was ruined by the fall of its tower 200 years ago. Previous to the fall of the tower it is recorded that – "the ravouns did stand thereon to soyle ye stepll goteris with bonys and other things," – and iron spikes were put on to prevent this; also that the bells were rung whenever there was a "gret thundering." Not far from St Mary's Church, down a narrow street, I came upon a wonderful piece of squared flint work, part of the wall of a stable-yard [Hamet St], as I make my way

69

to the third church in Sandwich, St Peter's. This church presents a very ruinous aspect both externally and internally, the tower having fallen a few years before that of St Mary's. I have much pleasure in recording the praiseworthy efforts of the vicar to restore it by the aid of offerings from visitors and others.

Fisher Gate, Sandwich

From here I pass the interesting market place, and then prepare for the journey back to Margate.

When returning through Sandwich follow the one-way system as follows:

From St Bartholomew's Hospital, cross the level crossing into New St. Passing the Guildhall on the left, bear right into Hamet St and continue to a 'T' junction. Turn right into Strand St to a 'T' junction. Turn left, go through the Barbican, over the river and out of Sandwich.

At the Barbican I am obliged to stop for a few minutes, for the drawbridge is open to permit the passage of a barge up the river; my vehicle is however free of the toll here charged.

Sandwich, circa 1890

Once over the River Stour I am in a part of the Isle of Thanet which is almost an island in itself. The Stour here forms a loop, and in this loop is situated all that remains of the rival of Sandwich in the Saxon period – the town of Stonar. The first farm house I pass on the right hand with its cottages close by is known as 'Little Stonar', and the second similar clump as 'Great Stonar'. These are the remnants of a once flourishing town. Away to my left can be seen the massive walls, covered with ivy, of Richborough Castle – the *Portus Ritupia* of the Romans.

Ruins of Richborough Castle

I now ride leisurely between two ditches containing water-lilies, the yellow flag and the reed mace (generally called bulrush). The surface of these ditches is clothed with duckweed and over them is flying in great plenty the little China Mark Moth, the curious aquatic larvae having food upon the duckweed. I pass by the salt pans, a relic of an age when salt was an expensive luxury, and ride on until I am close to the white cottages of the Coastguard Station. Here I turn off to Ebbsfleet on the left hand. A ride of a mile brings me to a level crossing on the S.E.R., and as I set off to the civility of the old pensioner who opens the gates, I purchase some of the roses which cover his cottage. A little further on, at Sevenscore, I take a road leading to Ramsgate, so directed by the signpost, and after passing under a railway bridge, stop to examine the Saxon cross erected by Earl Granville to mark the spot where St Augustine met King Ethelbert after he had landed at Ebbsfleet, A.D. 596. The cross is in every way worthy of the donor and the object it commemorates.

Sevenscore farmhouse

St Augustine's Cross, Ebbsfleet

From here I follow the road to Cliffsend – a beautiful road, with large evergreen shrubs on each side, and after due consideration decide to return to Margate by Ozengell and not by Manston. I walk up the hill known to cyclists as Staner's hill, and am near a Saxon cemetery opened up when the S.E.R. [South Eastern Railway] was made. At the top of the hill I turn round to admire the view, when to my great surprise the French coast is lit up by the setting sun and appears to be only five or six miles distant. The cliffs are clear and distinct, resembling those of Shanklin and the neighbourhood, and behind them lie what may be houses, one building appearing large like a factory. The whole scene is more like a mirage than anything it has been my lot to witness, and subsequent enquiries have proved that it was quite phenomenal. (Mem: Always carry a field glass). I have no doubt that others who saw the French coast on that day from either Ramsgate, Deal, or Dover can fix the date of this ramble thereby. I was loathe to turn away from the sight, and nothing on the rest of my journey had any interest for me.

"A soft and mellow sadness rose,
And tinged with earth the hues of heaven[7]"

---

[7] George Howard, Earl of Carlisle (Lord Morpeth), Stanzas (1831)

Modern directions for Ramble 2

From Margate's Turner Contemporary Art Gallery:

When starting this ramble one needs to travel up Margate's High Street from the harbour area. Parts of the High Street have been pedestrianised during certain times of the day, necessitating a dismount. On reaching St John's Church, at the end of the High Street, keep to the right of the church and enter the one-way system (A255) for about 100m to some crossroads. Bear right onto the Ramsgate Rd (A254, under the railway bridge (once the site of East Margate Station) and on to the traffic lights

Continue along the A256 Ramsgate Rd to a roundabout at Westwood Cross. Take the 3rd exit, onto the A256 Haine Rd

At the next roundabout take the 2nd exit (Haine Rd)

At the next roundabout take the 2nd exit also (Haine Rd)

At the double roundabout, take the 1st exit at the 1st roundabout and the 2nd exit at the next, into the A256 Sandwich Rd and past the Viking Ship and Pegwell Bay Nature Reserve

At the next roundabout take the 1st exit

At the next roundabout take the 2nd exit, towards Sandwich

At the next roundabout take the 1st exit, along the Ramsgate Rd

At the next roundabout take the 1st exit

At the next (small) roundabout, take the 2nd exit and on to the bridge into Sandwich

Follow the one-way system, around the Barbican into the High St, to a 'T' junction

Turn left into New St, and travel over the level crossing to a roundabout. Take the first exit onto the Deal Rd (A258)

Take the turning on the right signposted for Ham, to Ham Ponds

Return to the Deal Rd and turn left

Take the first turning on the left into Felderland Lane

At the staggered junction, turn left then immediate right into Sandwich Rd and on through Eastry

Take the cycle path on the right, about 50m before the roundabout, and continue until Tilmanstone is signposted on the right

After visiting Tilmanstone return to the cycle path, and back through Eastry

Turn left then immediately right at the staggered junction, on to Felderland Lane

Turn left at the 'T' junction then take the second exit off the roundabout, back to Sandwich

Passing St Bartholomew's, cross the level crossing into New St

Passing the Guildhall on the left, bear right into Hamet St and continue on to a 'T' junction

Turn right into Strand St to a 'T' junction

Turn left, go through the Barbican over the river and out of Sandwich, to a small roundabout. Take the first exit

Continue along the Ramsgate Road, to the next roundabout. Take the 2nd exit

Continue to the next roundabout. Take the 3rd exit, towards Ramsgate

Continue to the next roundabout. Take the 2nd exit

Continue to the next roundabout. Take the 1st exit, signposted to Ebbsfleet Farm. At the end of the road, join the cycle path on the right to Ebbsfleet Lane. Continue over the level crossing to the crossroads at Sevenscore, turn right into Cottington Rd

Passing St Augustine's Cross on the right, bear left into Foads Lane then bear right into Cliffs End Rd

Turn left at the 'T' junction onto the A256 Sandwich Rd and follow the signs back to Margate

RAMBLE 3

(Map 3)

Distance approximately 30 miles

Margate

Garlinge

Birchington

Acol

Monkton

Sheriff Court

Durlock

Ebbsfleet

Pegwell Bay

St Lawrence

Nethercourt

Northwood

Broadstairs

North Foreland

Reading Street

Northdown

Cliftonville

Margate

I am once more in the saddle, and the motto of the New York Bicycle Club suggests itself:

> *"Turn, turn, my wheel, turn round and round*
> *Without a pause, without a sound,*
> *So spins the flying world away"*[8]

On this ramble I have a companion with me, a visitor to the Isle of Thanet from the Midlands, who is interested in the historical reminiscences with which this island bounds, therefore the pronoun 'I' will be dropped for 'we'.

Our ride along the Marine Terrace is rather a jolting one, but improves as we pass the Royal Crescent.

Marine Terrace in 1868

Royal Crescent (Nayland Rock Hotel), Margate in the 1870s

---

[8] Henry Wadsworth Longfellow, Keramos, (1878)

At the Sea Bathing Infirmary we get a glimpse of the statue of Sir Erasmus Wilson.

Royal Sea Bathing Infirmary

We next climb Westbrook Bridge, and are soon at the hamlet of Garlinge. Here we are upon historic ground, for away to the right hand is a gap leading to the sea, where no fewer than 27 Bronze Age Celts were dug up close together many years ago. This of itself is sufficient proof that Thanet was occupied by the ancient inhabitants of Britain, and we can "in fancy descry the Briton in his wicker coracle paddling in calm weather in the shallow bays of the Isle of Thanet"[9].

On our left hand, immediately past the 'Hussar', is an interesting farmhouse, clothed for the most part with variegated ivy [previously known as Bethlehem Farm]. Next on our right is probably the finest bed of asparagus in the island. At St James's Church we alight and pay a visit to the ancient gateway of Dent-de-Lion. Close by the gateway a man is digging a pit into which we peer very closely, since near this spot some very curious Roman remains were once discovered, and we are willing to admit there is some truth in the following lines:

"Rare are the buttons of a Roman's breeches,
In antiquarian eyes surpassing riches,
That held of ancient Rome the flesh and fish"[10]

---

[9] James Robinson Planché, A Corner of Kent (Ash-next-Sandwich), 1864
[10] Peter Pindar, Peter's Prophecy or The President and Poet, (1788)

The original Hussar Hotel, Garlinge
This was replaced when the road was widened in the 1930s.

St James's Church, Garlinge

High Street, Garlinge

As we look round us we conclude that in place of belted knights the speciality of Dent-de-Lion is traction engines.

Victorian steam-driven traction engine 1891

Dent-de-Lion, Garlinge

Anxiety for the safety of our machines, however, hurries us from this interesting and umbrageous spot and we continue our ride along what was probably a Roman road or street, if we may judge from the names of the only two old houses in the modern fashionable resort of Westgate.

These two houses are close to the road, one on each side, embedded in trees, and were known as Street Court and Street Cottage. The former is covered with ivy, and has a well fitted-up entrance hall, but the latter is spoilt by a new villa frontage. From here we have a pleasant ride along an undulating road. We catch a glimpse of Westgate Church on our right, and get a good view of an ecclesiastical-looking tower, belonging to the waterworks, on our left.

Westgate-on-Sea water tower

82

We pass by retreats and villas, and reach Birchington Hall, with its pleasant avenue of trees, clean white front, and well-kept lawn. The Hall was formerly a farmhouse, with the road passing close to the entrance, and a pond situated between the elm trees now on the lawn and the roadway. A slight deviation of the road, the filling up of the pond, a new front to the Hall, enlargements in the rear, together with sheltered gardens and shrubberies have rendered this one of the most desirable residences in the island.

At the triangular piece of ground in Birchington yclept [called] the Square, we turn sharp to the left through a narrow lane somewhat dangerous to cyclists and are soon in the open country adjoining Quex Park. This is a famous place for the ornithologist. 'Hark, the lark at heaven's gate sings[11]' is exemplified on all sides of us. By the way this songster appears to be present all through the year and a warm day brings forth his melody. In the early summer the nightingale's song is heard here both night and day and many rare birds are occasional visitors in the Park, including the golden oriole.

Quex.

Quex House

The lives of the owners of Quex Park are recorded in the Crispe Chapel of Birchington Church, commencing with the ancient brass of old John Quck as follows:– *Hic jacet Johes Quck qui obiit xxi die Octobr A. Dni MCCCCXL IX* (the rest is mutilated). Formerly there was a road direct from the Park to Gore End, and probably the kidnappers of Henry Crispe took him along that road, now only a footpath remains.

With feet at rest we glide down a hill into the little hamlet of Acol, snug and sheltered, then we climb up nearly to Cleve Court, where we turn round to obtain a good view which includes the mansion and towers of Quex.

We are here reminded by the sight of a dilapidated old oak tree that Acol derives its name from the oaks which once covered this district, and the solitary

---

[11] Shakespeare's Cymbeline (1611)

83

specimen now before us might well have supplied the poet Spenser with the ideas in his beautiful but sad picture of an old oak tree:

"A huge oak, dry and dead
Still clad with reliques of its trophies old.
Lifting to heaven its ancient hoary head,
Whose foot on earth has got but slender hold.
And half disbowelled stands above the ground,
And trunk all rotten and unsound"[12]

Margate Road, Acol

On an excellent but uphill road we pass by the brick mansion of Cleve and its grove of trees, and alight at the top of the hill (Mount Pleasant) to examine the chalk pit, said to be the scene of Thunor's leap. We also attempt with a field glass to see the French coast, but no trace of it is visible, though we can discern with the naked eye the tower of Canterbury Cathedral and numerous church towers in the Stour valley.

---

[12] Edmund Spenser, The Ruins of Rome, (1591)

Cleve Court, Acol

From Mount Pleasant we get an enjoyable spin along a good road for more than two miles to Monkton.

Modern day cyclists can use the original road, which runs parallel to the dual carriageway

Before reaching the church my companion hurries off on the right to a conspicuous seamark, while I hunt up the keys. When I have succeeded in my object and reach the church I discover that he has arrived before me and is amusing himself with the stocks outside the churchyard.

The stocks outside Monkton Church

He reports that the 'seamark' is an uninteresting object at close quarters, resembling a Midland factory chimney built of brick, with a rough inscription giving the date of its restoration.

The seamark that stood near Monkton

This is now long gone. It was built in 1789 by the Corporation of the Trinity House, for the safety of navigation[13]. It was about ten feet in diameter and twenty-nine feet high, built with brick and capped with stone, and was built on the site of a former windmill. At around the time of WW1, Trinity House decided it was superfluous due to modern communications methods and should be demolished. The two local firms who tendered for the work, W.J. Cole and John Foreman Pettman, were related through marriage and "to avoid a family feud" they were commissioned to do the work together.

Monkton Church shows signs of having been built in more prosperous times (like St Nicholas) for the aisle on the north has disappeared, and the blocked up arches now form the wall of the nave. The interior is remarkable for its plainness. The chancel is almost level with the nave and formerly was a step lower, in striking contrast to more modern chancels with their numerous raised steps. After examining the well-known brass of the Monkton priest and that of the philanthropist, 'Libby Orchard', we climb up some ladders to the belfry and find that some of the bells are not hung. A portion of the tower is now used as the vestry, and in crossing the floor above the vestry our guide recommends us to take care to step on the joists since a short time previously a ludicrous accident occurred. At a wedding (an uncommon occurrence now at Monkton) a man took up his position surreptitiously at a grating over the vestry to watch the ceremony.

---

13 A Topographical Dictionary of England, Samuel Lewis, 1840, p. 293. Mockett's Journal, 1836, p. 31

When it was over the clergyman retired to disrobe, and at the same time the man above began to cross the floor. In so doing he slipped, and the clergyman below being alarmed by falling plaster, looked up just in time to see a pair of legs come through the ceiling. Fortunately an intervening beam prevented his coming bodily through but there he hung until released.

We have another pleasant ride through the pretty village of Monkton, then turn to the right to look at Sheriff Court (another improved farmhouse), and to save going back we push our machines along a footpath which leads to Minster railway station.

Low lying branches may be hazardous to cyclists along this rough footpath, which runs alongside the river. To avoid the footpath take the following route: Return along Sheriff's Court Lane to the Monkton Road. Turn right to Minster and turn right into the High St, at the bottom of which is Minster Church.

Minster Church is so well known that I need only mention one or two of the characteristics most prominent to our minds. Outside we note the sundial, the Norman turret, the curious flying buttresses, and the numerous monuments to the 'Swinford' family. The interior strikes us as exceptionally fine, as does the carving on the Miserere seats, but it is an immense disappointment to find no chained bible and so little trace of it, for the existence of such a bible at Minster Church was almost an article of our creed.

Church Street, Minster

The Bell Inn, Minster

Next we proceed through the village of Minster as far as Buddle's tea gardens where we obtain the 'cyclist's best meal' – a pot of tea and etceteras, made more enjoyable by pleasant floral surroundings.

The New Inn, Minster
The building in the middle of the picture is the New Inn, circa 1900. It was here that Buddle's Tea Gardens flourished.

After this refreshment we return to the church, passing on our way some very old houses with carved stones in out of the way places, these stones probably having formed part of the old conventional building.

Minster, with the church in the background

At St Mildred's Abbey, the oldest inhabited house in Thanet, we peep through the railings at a respectful distance, and then try unsuccessfully to obtain a view of the interior through a side gate. We endeavour to console ourselves by admiring the beautiful avenue of trees which form the entrance to Minster from Ramsgate and next decide to proceed to Ebbsfleet.

Minster Abbey, also known as St Mildred's

One of those 'contretemps' to which the cyclist is frequently liable now occurs. We take out our ordnance map, scale one inch to a mile, the latest published, and a road is plainly shown thereon leading from Minster to Ebbsfleet via Durlock. We follow it past several very old cottages. As we proceed in the direction of the S.E.R. the road gradually becomes worse until at Durlock it dwindles down to a mere footpath, a very pleasant footpath withal, having a hedge on each side. We are able to ride along it, grass grown as it is, for about half a mile when suddenly it terminates in a turnip field. The labourers at work advise us to cross the field and to remove some hurdles at the opposite side in order to get into the road to Ebbsfleet, and one of them informs us that in his father's time this was a carriage road. We follow the advice given, and are soon upon a hard road and on historic ground, Ebbsfleet, with a distant view of St Augustine's cross.

Durlock Lodge

The route from Minster to Ebbsfleet via Durlock no longer exists, neither does the old village of Durlock as shown on the old map. To continue the route:

From Church St, pass Conyngham Rd on the right and then turn right at Durlock Lodge, into Durlock. Follow this dead end road, which turns into a concrete track, to the railway line. Cross the line and turn left along a grass track. (It was here that our cyclist continued straight on through Durlock to Ebbsfleet, as shown on the old map.) Continue along the grass track, pass through a large iron field-gate and on to Ebbsfleet Lane at which, turn right. At the A256 Sandwich Road, turn left.

By following the pretty country lane we get to the Coastguard Station near Pegwell Bay, its white cottages being a conspicuous landmark; we skirt Pegwell Bay, hurry up the hill to the Ramsgate road, and peddle on to St Lawrence leaving Nethercourt on our left. At St Laurence Church there are three objects we desire to see – first, the brass of Nicholas Manstone, Armiger, A.D. 1444, since he wears the noted S S collar, the origin of which is still open to doubt; second, the quaint heads (one gagged) upon the pier caps and from which the vicar has founded an amusing allegory; and, third, the tomb of Mrs Froude (wife of the historian). After satisfying our curiosity and examining other points of interest we proceed on our ramble.

St Lawrence

St Laurence Church

Leaving Ramsgate on our right, we cross the S.E.R. bridge, go through Northwood, and so on to the pretty village of St Peter's with its fine elm trees and handsome church. We leave our machines at the C.T. [Cyclists' Touring] house, the Wheat Sheaf, after entering our names in their visitor's book, and then look round the church and churchyard. We search in vain for an epitaph said to be here:

"Here lies the body of –
Who was drowned at sea and never found"

But we come across a curious one to the Kentish Samson which ends as follows:

"Death comes to all
Goliath great and David small"

And also notice a brass in the church inscribed to Richard Culmer 'Carpenterias'.

St Peter's seems to have been a place of some importance a century ago, since Mockett records that in 1786 "Umbrellas were used by three or four persons in St Peter's."

We now remount and hasten down the hill to Broadstairs, up another hill out of the town and on without stopping to the North Foreland Lighthouse. The keeper shows us the beautiful lenses of the lantern and explains its working, and this sight alone would have fully compensated us for the time spent on our ramble. We ask him concerning the migration of birds as observed by the light of the lantern, and he becomes quite eloquent upon the flocks of birds at certain seasons of the year which cross the light, and of the poor unfortunates which frequently strike the lantern and are thereby injured.

Broadstairs 1890

North Foreland Lighthouse

It is now time to finish our ramble, so we return from the lighthouse to Stone House and Callis Grange (an old 15th century house), and then make our way to Reading Street for the purpose of looking at the numerous gable ends of cottages, of the time of William III. Some of them are exceeding quaint in design. We pass within a short distance of a sea-mark, also a monument, and then arrive at Northdown. We have pleasant recollections of the house and grounds of Northdown, of hares in the park where they are safe from the pursuit of their natural enemies, of violets in the shrubberies, of the fine sea views from the summer-house and of feathered songsters everywhere.

Whitfield Tower
The seamark referred to near Northdown was erected in 1818 and fell down during a storm in 1979.

93

We follow the road towards Margate and slacken our pace to watch the sun go down into the silver sea, such a sunset as would have delighted the great artist Turner.

Through Cliftonville past St Paul's and Trinity Churches, our ramble is ended, and I conclude with a translation by the late vicar of Monkton of a Latin couplet formerly in that church, which seems appropriate for the purpose:

"Thanet, that island round, which waters bound,
So sound, with fruits so crowned, what second can be found?"

Northdown Road, Cliftonville, circa 1910
This photograph shows St Paul's Church in the background.

Modern directions for Ramble 3

From Margate's Turner Contemporary Art Gallery:

Travel along the seafront on the B2051 (Marine Drive) towards the clock tower

Turn right onto the A254 (Marine Terrace)

At the roundabout take the 3rd exit, onto the A28 (Canterbury Rd), and follow this road to the roundabout at Birchington

Take the 1st exit and then turn immediately left, into Park Lane (B2048)

Continue along the B2048 for about 2½ miles, passing through Acol, to a roundabout

Take the 2nd exit and continue on to the next roundabout (Minster Roundabout)

Take the 3rd exit onto the A299 (Canterbury Rd West)

After about 150m take the road on the left (the original old road which runs parallel to the modern dual carriageway)

At the 'T' junction turn right to the roundabout and take the 1st exit (A253)

In about 400m there is a cross roads. Turn left here into Monkton St (This road, opposite Orchard Lane, is closed to vehicles, but accessible by bicycle and on foot)

Continue along Monkton St, past the White Stag public house, to a turning on the right called Sheriff's Court Lane

At the end of the road, there are public footpath signs. Take the footpath by the river. [Beware of low lying branches along this rough footpath, which runs alongside the river. To avoid the footpath take the following route: Return along Sheriff's Court Lane to the Monkton Rd. Turn right to Minster and turn right into the High St, at the bottom of which is Minster Church]

The footpath leads into Watchester Lane at the end of which, turn left into Station Rd

After about 200m turn right into Church St

Continue along Church St for about 400m then turn right into the dead end road called Durlock. This leads onto a footpath to a railway crossing

Cross the railway and turn left along the footpath to a 'T' junction

Turn right into Ebbsfleet Lane, until reaching a cycle path. Continue to a roundabout at which, take the 2nd exit, onto the A256 Sandwich Rd

At the next roundabout, take the 2nd exit onto the A299 (Canterbury Rd East)

At the next roundabout take the 2nd exit onto the A253

At the next roundabout take the 1st exit into Nethercourt Hill

At the roundabout in St Lawrence take the 1st exit into Newington Rd

Cross a mini roundabout and two sets of traffic lights, into Northwood Rd

At the roundabout take the 2nd exit onto the A256 Westwood Rd

At the next roundabout take the 1st exit (Asda on the right)

At the next roundabout, take the 2nd exit into Vicarage St

Turn right down the High St, opposite St Peter's Church

Turn left at the junction into The Broadway

Continue towards Broadstairs, crossing over the traffic lights and under the railway bridge

Continue straight ahead before bearing left into Albion St and on to Stone Rd, which becomes North Foreland Rd

North Foreland Lighthouse is on the left

Return along North Foreland Rd to a turning on the right called Lanthorne Rd

At the end of Lanthorne Rd turn right into Callis Court Rd, and take a turning on the left called Reading St

Go straight over the crossroads into Reading Street Rd

Turn right at the 'T' junction and then left onto Northdown Park Rd

Turn right down Foreland Avenue to the 'T' junction

Turn left into Northdown Rd, bearing left down Trinity Hill

Turn right into King St and return to Turner Contemporary

RAMBLE 4

(Maps 3, 4, 5)

Distance approximately 55 miles

Margate

Sandwich

Upper Deal

Deal

Walmer

Kingsdown

Cap Point

Deal

Upper Deal

Great Mongeham

Little Mongeham

Waldershare

Eythorne

Barfrestone

Fredville Park

Wingham Well

Ickham

Wickhambreaux

Grove Ferry

Margate

Ingoldsby's house, Margate in 1884

One may fairly be pardoned for drifting into admiration of the ever fresh and ever beautiful volume which nature's hand daily unfolds to the 'rambler' whose headquarters are at Margate, and one may also be accused for occasionally speaking in praise of the iron steed which enables him to visit, with ease and safety, the various places of interest in the neighbourhood. In the words of the poet Chaucer:

> *"This stede of bras, that esily and wel,*
> *Can in a space of a day naturel*
> *(That is to say in four and twenty houres),*
> *Wher so you list, in draught or elles shoures,*
> *Baren your body, into every place,*
> *To which your herte willeth for to pace."*[14]

Upon this, my fourth ramble, my companion is a lady cyclist, and our start is delayed until two o'clock in the afternoon for the arrival of a third cyclist, who, however, fails to appear, and sends telegram instead. We take the Sandwich road, as described in ramble No 2; quietly and steadily we jog along, side by side when the road is clear, and in Indian file whenever any vehicle meets us; we get up a fair rate of speed along the level; we put our feet at rest as our machines carry us

---

[14] Chaucer, The Squire's Tale

rapidly down the hills, and as we pass the 'saltpans' we even venture to try to keep in front of some rather awkward bicyclists, who only succeed, after most frantic efforts, in getting ahead of us just as we reach the drawbridge at Sandwich, at half-past three o'clock. We rest at Sandwich for half an hour, and then take the road to Deal.

To negotiate the modern one-way system, turn left and around the Barbican into the High St. Follow the one-way system to a 'T' junction. Turn left into New St and follow this road over the level crossing to a roundabout. Take the first exit onto the Deal Rd.

We pass St Bartholomew's Hospital at the outskirts of Sandwich, and here I could, with your permission, thank the Rev. H Gilder for setting me right concerning the state of the chapel of the hospital. I rejoice that it has been restored to its proper use, and cordially agree with him in the hope that the present owner of Salmestone (who is, I believe, a member of the Kent Archaeological Society) will imitate so good an example.

The bridge at Sandwich

The Deal road is in fair condition, and as we travel along it at the rate of something like six miles an hour, we have a pleasant ride, through fields of corn, clover, and sweet-scented beans in blossom. On our right hand is rising ground to Northbourne, where was a large camp when the Spanish Armada was daily expected, and on our left hand are the sand hills, with the signal batteries (now Coastguard Stations), while out in the Downs may be seen some large merchant vessels. We can here picture the ancient inhabitants of Kent as they gazed upon the ships of old Rome sailing in with the tide, or as they bravely threw their lives away in defence of their 'homes and country' against a disciplined foe. A slight descent and we have a ditch on each side of us, and we cross a narrow stream, a fine locality for 'early' celery, and assuredly we notice some that must be the very earliest in the market. We leave Sholden on our left, go through Upper Deal on a macadamised road, mount the steep ascent of the bridge over the railway, cross the High street, pass through a narrow lane, and dismount on the promenade at Deal.

Northbourne House
This is now a private school.

The Parade, Deal

It is now five o'clock, so we make our way to the touring house, 'The Black Horse', and our 'cloth[15]' obtains for us a hearty welcome and immediate attention; machines are stowed away and by the time we have removed the dust from ourselves we are informed that 'tea is waiting'.

The Black Horse, Deal
Note the cyclist on a tricycle on the road outside – could he be ours…?

After tea my companion suggests a further ride, to Kingsdown and back; so our machines are brought out again, and we set off. We pass Deal Castle and the barracks; also great heaps of shingle, a wonderful sight in themselves, but rendered more striking by the roar of the sea as the waves dash against the shore.

---

[15] Probably a reference to the uniform of the Cyclists' Touring Club: dark green/grey Devonshire serge jacket, knickerbockers and a "Stanley helmet with a small peak"

Deal Castle

Soon we reach Walmer, and the beautiful grounds surrounding Walmer Castle, a place rich with memories of Palmerstone, Wellington, Pitt, and other noteworthy wardens of the Cinque Ports. From Walmer Castle to Kingsdown we have a bank on our right hand with wild flowers thereon too numerous to enumerate. It is getting towards sunset, yet the Marbled White butterfly is still floating from flower to flower, the Little Blues are settling themselves to rest on the long stems of grass, and Burnet Moths may be picked off the flowers in abundance. I stop a few minutes to take notes of the lepidopteron, and then hurry on to overtake my companion.

Walmer Castle

The Promenade, Walmer

The Promenade at Walmer

When we reach Kingsdown, which is a little fishing hamlet, we leave our machines and walk further on to the tall white cliffs. A pathway under the cliffs can be followed as far as St Margaret's Bay, but we return at 'Cap' Point.

The space between the cliffs and the sea is covered with herbage, one of the most conspicuous plants being the hemp agrimony, which grows here in great plenty and when in bloom is very attractive to insects. Formerly the London entomologists journeyed hither in search of a beautiful and rare moth, *Plusia Orichalcea*, the scarce Burnished Brass, and many other rare lepidoptera have been obtained in this locality, but now the hemp agrimony is not in blossom.

Kingsdown

As we return, a yellow patch in the shingle attracts our attention and accordingly we make our way towards it across the stones. In doing so, our footfalls are strangely echoed from the cliffs, and we also notice how clearly can be heard the voices of some men in a fishing boat at a great distance, together with the answering echo. The yellow patch proves to be the flowers of the yellow horned poppy, *glancium luteum,* apparently growing out of the stones, but really growing out of the sand below. The flower is as beautiful as the field poppy, and, like that flower, its petals fall quickly, but it differs in having no scent. We gather a bunch, and also pull up by the roots a specimen of the sea holly, *eryngium maritinum*. Next we satisfy our curiosity by examining the 'dummy' soldiers set up to be fired at, and then return to Kingsdown.

Kingsdown Ranges 1896

A ride of half-an-hour suffices to take us back to Deal, not without reminders on the way that 'our wheels are going round' and enquiries as to the whereabouts of our lamps. We finish the evening with a walk on the promenade and beach, where we watch the boatmen winding up their boats – a fresh experience for my companion.

Deal Promenade 1890
Notice the winch on the right, used by the boatmen for 'winding up their boats'.

At breakfast next morning in the snug coffee-room, old fashioned and with curious crannies and nooks, we compare notes with a couple of tourists who are making a round of the towns on the south east coast by rail and it is unanimously voted that the road is more pleasant than the rail. At half past nine we leave the comfortable touring-house, take the road to Upper Deal and strike off to Great Mongeham. An opportunity offers for us to see the interior of the church and we avail ourselves of it. It is evidently of Norman origin since there is a Norman window in the north chancel. A square opening in the south chancel is pointed out to us as having formerly been used by lepers who stood outside. From the frequency of these openings one is led to think leprosy was a common disease with our forefathers, or that they were used for some other purpose. Our national vanity would prefer the latter. The old rood screen and a curious double piscina are worthy of examination.

View looking north, down Mill Road, Upper Deal, circa 1900

Great Mongeham

'The Friendly Port', Great Mongeham

Our motto is, not 'Excelsior[16]' but 'Barfrestone' and we follow the nearest road through Little Mongeham. Soon we have a plantation on our left hand, not an advantage today since it keeps from us a pleasant breeze. As we approach the Dover road, which we cross at right angles, we begin to descend into a very pretty valley with the trees of Waldershare on our left and Tilmanstone on our right. The opposite side of the valley necessitates a dismount and we walk leisurely up the hill, then on to Eythorne with more hills. The road we travel is narrow, apparently little used and occasionally encumbered with loose stones. For several miles we meet no vehicle and it is evident, whenever we pass roadside cottages, that lady cyclists are not often seen in these parts.

At Eythorne we enter a district of beautiful lanes and tall and wide hedgerows, one disadvantage being that to pass a vehicle in them it is necessary to go back to a gateway. We reach Barfrestone about eleven o'clock and find a new companion waiting for us. First of all we obtain some non-alcoholic refreshment at the little 'off licensed' beer shop, where the keys of the church are kept, temperance principles being by far away the best for cyclists on a tour, especially in the early part of the day. Then our fresh companion having already been over the church acts as our guide, and describes its chief attractions. This gem of a church consists of a chancel and nave, the whole being no larger than a good sized drawing room. The chancel is 16 ½ ft by 13 ½ ft, and nave 37 ft by 16 ½ ft and it has no tower. The pulpit is placed at the west end, and there are seats for forty or fifty worshippers. Our self-appointed guide grows eloquent upon the beauty of the

---

[16] The catchphrase of Dr Ferguson in Jules Verne's adventure story "Five Weeks in a Balloon", published 1863

interior, its elaborate stone carving, the curious Norman ornament known as the Greek key which runs round the walls, and the fine Norman chancel arch.

We take a rough sketch of the east end window and then examine the exterior with its sculptured figures. It is a beautiful little church, which has been well restored by Sir Gilbert Scott, and we are reluctant to leave it. Before doing so we enquire its history of the custodian of the keys, who tells us that nothing is known of its erection and that the British Museum contains no record of it. Subsequently we discover that there exists a 'conjecture' which may account for the presence of so much carved stonework in this rural edifice. The conjecture is that we owe this church to the ambition of Archbishop Baldwin and the jealousy of the monks of Christ Church Canterbury. Baldwin becomes Archbishop of Canterbury in 1186, and determined to erect a rival monastery at Hackington. The monks appeal to both the Crown and the Pope, who prohibited the erection of the new building, but in spite of all opposition the work was completed. In the year 1190 the Archbishop died on a crusade in the Holy Land, and at once the rival monastery was destroyed, and it may have been that the materials used were removed to Barfrestone. The date of its architecture is suitable and evidence is forthcoming that the stonework at Barfrestone had been previously built into some erection which had a very short existence.

Barfrestone Church

We make a detour to a beautiful old house with an elaborate carved front and thatched roof and regret we cannot spare time to ask permission to view the interior. Then in order to escape a rough piece of road, we enter through the gateway of Fredville Park, as advised, and ride over the short turf. In the words of Chaucer:

108

"We come to a land of white and green,
So fair a one we had never in been,
The ground was green y-powdered with daisy,
The flowers and the groves alike high
All green and white was nothing else seen."[17]

We pass close by the house and the well-trimmed lawn reminds us of the same poet's picture of a garden:

"Well y-wrought with turfes newe,
Freshly turved, whereof the grene gras,
So small, so thicke, so shorte, so fresh of hewe,
That most like unto grene wool, wot we, it was."[18]

Overlooking the Park is the 'Cricketers'[19]. Dinner was just over, one o'clock; they had nothing in the house but they would send to the butcher's half a mile off. To save time, our companion volunteered to go on his bicycle. We have an enjoyable meal, the ozone we have inhaled giving a zest to the appetite and cheerfulness to the spirits.

The old oak tree at Fredville Park
The tree is believed to be over 1200 years old.

---

[17] Chaucer, The Month of May (taken from Chaucer's Dream)
[18] Chaucer, The Leaf, from The Flower and the Leaf
[19] Until the early 1960's 'The Oak' Public House, which overlooks Fredvill Park, had a tea garden, serving both cricketers using the ground opposite and the general public from a building at the end of the garden. This may well have been our cyclist's 'Cricketers'. www.nonington.co.uk

We take the nearest road to Wingham; we are told it is 'turrible rough', but don't find it so, and we get over the ground quickly, our lady cyclist having the advantage of being pushed up all big hills. At Wingham our only stoppage is at the noted well, where we drink of the renowned water, which is very refreshing. Chaucer might have described this well when he wrote:

> *"The gravel golden, the water pure as glass,*
> *The bank is round the well environing,*
> *And soft as velvet was the young grass.*
> *That thereupon hastily came springing,*
> *The suit of trees, abouten compassing,*
> *Their shadow cast, closing the wall around.*
> *And all the herb is growing on the ground."*[20]

Old windmill at Wingham Well

The road here is in perfect condition for cycling and the trees are a pleasant shelter as we ride side by side to a signpost which illustrates the Saxon names of the district. It points forward to Ickham and Wickham and backwards to Wingham. At Ickham we pass an old Tudor gateway at a brewery and at Wickhambreaux we stop to watch the revolutions of a waterwheel at a mill on the Little Stour River – an excellent example of an undershot wheel. I quit my companions and cross the large and shaded village green to look into the open church. It is carefully restored and its wall paintings, pews, and floor tiles give it a modern appearance. The east-end window is dwarfed by the height of the altar and gives one the idea that the chancel and nave were formerly on the same level.

---

[20] Chaucer, The Complaint of the Black Knight, from The Book of the Duchess or Chaucer's Dream

Ickham Church

Water mill at Wickhambreaux
This is now a private residence.

The solitary brass on the chancel wall is inscribed:

*"Hic jacet dns Henricus Welde quouia Rector isti Ecclie qui obiit nons die
Octobris, Anno dni MCCCXX. Cui aie ppicietur deus. Amen.21"*

The effigy is missing and has probably shared the fate of those of a very elaborate character at Ickham Church, whose Matrices are 'in situ'.

The old Post Office at Wickhambreaux

The Forge, Wickhambreaux

---

[21] According to www.kentarchaeology.org.uk/Research/Libr/MIs/MIsWickambreaux the
inscription reads: '*Hic jacet Dns Henricus Welde quond Rector isti Eccle qui obiit nono die
Octobris Anno Dni MCCCCXX. Cui aie ppicietur Deus. Amen*'. Note the conflicting date.

A smart run of two miles over a rather loose road brings us to Grove and we cross the marshes to the ferry, passing close to the lavender gardens, which, by their sweet but almost overpowering perfume remind us of the renowned Mitcham gardens, where oil of lavender realised £1 per pint bottle. We order a large pot of tea at the Ferry House, open wide the window, draw up the table thereto and watch the ferry boat as it crosses and re-crosses the Stour.

Grove Ferry Inn
This is the Ferry House referred to above.

Grove Ferry

The toll for each passenger on the ferry boat is a halfpenny and a similar sum is charged for our machines as we cross. We walk over the level crossing on the S.E.R. and push our machines up the steep hill (dangerous ride down) to the Canterbury main road.

Then as we proceed towards Margate the sentiment that it is:

"Passing sweet to ramble, free as air
Blithe truants in the bright and breeze blessed day,
Far from the town!" [22]

is unanimously adopted by our little party of three and a south-west breeze helps us very materially to conclude our journey pleasantly.

---

[22] Henry Walker, Saturday afternoon rambles round London, 1871

Modern directions for Ramble 4

From Margate's Turner Contemporary Art Gallery:

When starting this ramble one needs to travel up Margate's High Street from the harbour area. Parts of the High Street have been pedestrianised during certain times of the day, necessitating a dismount. On reaching St John's Church, at the end of the High Street, keep to the right of the church and enter the one-way system (A255) for about 100m to some crossroads. Bear right onto the Ramsgate Rd (A254), under the railway bridge (once the site of East Margate Station) and on to the traffic lights

Continue along the A256 Ramsgate Rd to a roundabout at Westwood Cross. Take the 3rd exit, onto the A256 Haine Rd

Continue along the Haine Rd, across 2 roundabouts, to a double roundabout

Take the 1st exit at the 1st roundabout and the 2nd exit at the next, into the A256 Sandwich Rd and past the Viking Ship and Pegwell Bay Nature Reserve

At the next roundabout take the 1st exit

At the next roundabout take the 2nd exit, towards Sandwich

At the next roundabout take the 1st exit, along the Ramsgate Rd

At the next roundabout take the 1st exit

At the next (small) roundabout, take the 2nd exit and on to the bridge into Sandwich

Follow the one-way system, around the Barbican into the High St, to a 'T' junction

Turn left into New St and over the level crossing to a roundabout. Take the first exit onto the Deal Rd (A258) and continue through Deal, over the railway line to the High Street, to the Black Horse Hotel

Continue to the sea front, turn right along the promenade all the way to Kingsdown

Return to Deal

From the Black Horse, return along the A258 to Sholden

At Sholden turn left into Mongeham Rd and head through Little Mongeham. Turn right into Boys Hill to the main A256 roundabout

Take the 2nd exit, into Barville Rd, which becomes Wigmore Lane

Passing Shooter's Hill on the left, turn right into Church Hill

Continue to a fork in the road and take the left fork into Barfreston Rd and hence through Barfreston

Take the second right, after Pie Factory Rd, into Nightingale Lane (no street sign), which becomes Butter St then Chapmans Hill then Ratling Rd

At the 'T' junction turn right, onto the B2046 Adisham Rd

Turn left into Wingham Well Lane

Turn right into Watercress Lane

Turn right into Mill Rd

Turn right onto the A257 then immediately left into Wingham Rd, which becomes The Street

Bear right into Wickham Lane

At the 'T' junction turn right into Wickham Rd

Bear left into Wickham Court Lane

Bear right into Grove Rd and up Grove Ferry Hill to the 'T' junction

Turn right onto the A28 Island Rd and continue to Margate

RAMBLE 5

(Maps 3, 4, 7)

Distance approximately 35 miles

Margate

Westgate-on-Sea

Birchington

Sarre

Westbere

Sturry

Fordwich

Stodmarsh

Grove Ferry

Margate

Margate clock tower

In these days of eager touring to distant shores in search of new sensations, it is not an unwholesome lesson to learn that:

> *"For things far off we tell, whilst many a good*
> *Not sought, because too near, is never gained."*[23]

In my previous rambles I have shown how much mental entertainment lies at our very doors, amidst rural landscapes, which, upon the authority of an eminent naturalist and traveller, far surpass in beauty those of the tropical regions. Dr Wallace[24] writes as follows: "I have never seen in the tropics such brilliant masses of colour as Kent can show in her furze-clad commons, her patches of heather, her glades of wild hyacinths and primroses, her meadows of buttercups and orchids, her fields of poppies and of clover – carpets of yellow, purple, azure blue, and fiery crimson which the tropics can rarely exhibit. Our hawthorn and crab trees, our holly and mountain ash, our broom, foxglove and purple vetches, clothe with gay colour the length and breadth of the county. These beauties are all common, they have not to be sought for, they are characteristic of the land and gladden the eye at every step, whilst in the region of the equator a sombre green clothes universal nature, flowers are everywhere rare and anything at all striking is only to be met with at very rare intervals."

Upon the occasion of this my fifth ramble out of Margate, my visitor from the Midlands accompanies me, as he desires to enjoy the pleasure of another ride in

---

[23] William Wordsworth, The River Eden, Cumberland, during a tour in the summer of 1833
[24] Alfred Russel Wallace (1823–1913) was a British naturalist, explorer, geographer, anthropologist and biologist.

the pure atmosphere of Thanet and East Kent before returning to the smoke of the town of 'hardware'.

Taking the Canterbury road as previously described we soon reach Westgate and stop there sufficient time to see an aloe in blossom, exhibited for the benefit of a local charity.

Westgate-on-Sea

Then on to Birchington where we make a second stoppage. As we descend a slope out of the village we find, in a garden close to the road, a couple of ancient fig trees and the occupier of the garden assures us that one of them is over a hundred years old. It has a fair quantity of fruit on it, while its very existence for such a long period speaks highly for the mildness of the winters in the favoured Isle of Thanet. In this spot a successful florist and grower of early fruit has established himself, and a few yards further on, opposite the great pond, we notice several fine specimens of a tropical plant, the eucalyptus, growing most luxuriously in a gentleman's garden without any protection whatsoever from the winter frosts, and the owner of these uncommon plants shows to us, with pardonable pride, some gigantic calceolarias in magnificent blossom, which have lived out of doors without any protection through several winters – a sufficient proof in themselves that the proximity of the sea tempers the severity of the frosts. As we remount our machines we glance at the village of Birchington, which makes from here a very pretty picture.

119

A view from Birchington Square, showing the road to Margate, circa 1890

We ride on to Sarre, through fields green with corn in blossom, or radiant with poppies and clover and gardens where the young hops are hastening up the tall poles and on Sarre Wall we stop at a fine avenue of trees:

"Here grows the tree where rolled the deep.
Oh, earth! What changes hast thou seen."[25]

King's Head, Sarre
This is now a private residence.

---

[25] Alfred, Lord Tennyson, In Memoriam. Original reads:
'There rolls the deep where grew the tree.
O earth, what changes hast thou seen!'

Before us are some fine aspens, every leaf in a constant state of agitation. We alight and pluck some of the leaves to see the cause of the quivering movement, which is simply that the stalk is slender and does not form a rigid support, but permits the leaf to dangle from it like the hand of a weak wrist and hence the leaf becomes the sport of airs which are impalpable to the firmly supported leaves of other trees.

Half way across Sarre Wall, the River Stour, in its meanderings from Sandwich towards Canterbury, approaches close to the road, and we pay a visit to the ferry. As we stand on the river's bank, the wide stretching space that opens before us is almost prairie-like in extent:

> "The grass, the elm, the blossomed thorn
> Those cattle crouching, and as they rise
> Their shining flanks and liquid eyes – " [26]

– together with the smock-clad shepherd and his shaggy dog, give a pastoral air to the whole scene.

The road from Sarre Wall is somewhat loose, but we plough through it up the hill and when we reach the top an improvement takes place. We bowl along at a rapid pace on the good hard surface, several miles here being excellent, whenever there is a favourable breeze, for the making of records. Today we are not desirous of breaking a previous record and we stop at a plantation at the roadside where part of the timber has been felled, and the undergrowth is about a year old. The ground is literally covered with the 'ragged robin', its pink flowers giving colour to the scene. In the stumps of the oak trees are to be found in plenty the larvae of the Hyde-Park Clear-Wing Moth *(Secia Cynipiformis)*, which was formerly considered to be very scarce, and only to be found in Hyde Park, but now when its habits are known, the entomologist meets with it in every Kentish oak wood, the year after the felling of the trees.

A short distance further on the road towards Canterbury, we turn to the left and by a narrow and steep descent we come to the interesting little village of Westbere. It lies snugly sheltered from the north winds and consists of church, mansion, farm houses, ancient cottages and tall elm trees close together and is nearly surrounded by hop gardens. An air of quiet content pervades the whole place. The church is an ancient structure, well restored, the walls having recently being faced with flints and the interior re-pewed, making it in complete accord with the rest of the village. Its three bells are open to view in the little bell turret and we learn from an old inhabitant that Stodmarsh Church, which stands on the opposite side of the River Stour has two bells only and that on Sundays the bells of Westbere ring out plainly:

> *We ring the best, we ring the best,*

And the answer across the marshes from Stodmarsh is:

> *We too, we too, we too*

---

[26] Matthew Arnold, Epilogue to Lessing's Laocoön

Westbere Church and its three-bell turret

The Yew Tree Inn, Westbere

We rejoin the high-road at Stains Hill and soon arrive at the level crossing on the South Eastern Railway at Sturry. A feature of Sturry is the cultivation of sunflowers, which grow here most luxuriantly, and in many gardens we notice also a tall kind of balsam. The most striking trees are tall poplars and willows. The church is of varied architecture, the aisles being built long after the nave. The arcades have been cut out of the ancient wall, leaving square pillars and the clerestory arches above have been filled in with masonry.

High Street, Sturry

Near the church we pass under a Tudor archway and then go through the village and over a couple of bridges to the ancient borough or city of Fordwich.

Sturry Church and Tudor Archway

We decide to make a considerable stay here for the double purpose of seeing as much as possible of this interesting spot and for refreshment. We visit the old Guildhall, climb up into the ancient chamber, where the freemen and burgesses formerly met, for we are told the Charter of the Borough[27] has recently been taken away. We examine with great interest an ancient implement formerly used for the punishment of refractory women, known as the cucking stool, and other relics of bygone ages and we listen to the explanations given by our guide, who tells us of the ancient custom of the borough, including the right to catch fish at certain seasons and we learn from him that the freedom of Fordwich was more expensive than that of the City of London. The keys, the chest and the prison under the hall are found worthy of examination and an hour passes pleasantly in gossip with an 'old man eloquent' concerning the building of which he has charge.

Fordwich Old Guildhall

---

[27] Henry III granted Fordwich a Borough Charter, a status it maintained until 1886.

'Cucking' Stool, Fordwich

The Fordwich Arms

Next we make our way to the church and secure the services of another useful guide. In this my fifth ramble out of Margate this is the first village church I have seen which has altogether failed to derive benefit from the love of church restoration of the present age. The thick and rough walls are coloured on the interior with Paris blue, whilst the uneven floor and high-backed square pews suffice to carry one's mind back to a period when neglect of churches was the rule, but happily we live in better days and now Fordwich Church is an exception. There is one aisle on the north and the pillars between it and the nave are thick square blocks of masonry, apparently cut out of the old wall of the nave. In the aisle there is an old stone coffin without name or date and in the nave is a most beautiful brass, with this inscription:

"Here lyeth buryed ye body of Aphra Hawkins,
wife of Henry Hawkins, gent, and daughter of
Thomas Norton Esq., who scarcely having arrived
to 21 years of age, yet fully attayned perfection
in many virtues.
Departed this frayle life ye XVI of Janry, 1606."

The lady's effigy is in an excellent state of preservation, the dress has a very elaborately embroidered front, and the bodice is laced similar to the fashion of the present day. Such a dress must have been very costly, as the following bill for a young lady's dress made in a neighbouring town in the year 1594 will show:–

Item p'd for 2 yardes of violet broadcloth to make her a gown	xxiiijs	[24s]
Item p'd for 2 yardes of baise at 1 y'de cotton vjs	viijd	[8d]
Item p'd for divers things to furnish her gowne	xxixs	[29s]
Item p'd for makinge her gowne and styffinge to yt	vjs.iiijd	[6s 4d]

A total of £3, a large sum when we consider that the same young lady paid for board and lodgings 2s per week only.

A peculiar feature of Fordwich Church is the possession of two copies of the Decalogue[28], one in the usual position in the chancel, and the second over the chancel arch, where, our guide tells us, it was placed to give satisfaction to King William III, who worshipped here and desired this to be done in imitation of the custom existing in Holland.

---

[28] The Ten Commandments

The George and Dragon, Fordwich

The River Stour at Fordwich

On leaving Fordwich, we push our machines up a hill, the roadway full of ruts, with a high bank on either side and overhanging bushes. At the top of the hill we turn to the left on an excellent road and in a short time enter a very fine wood. Here is nature's temple with the long drawn aisles and fretted vaults and sweet side chapels, which tempt our feet from the highway on which we travel to the soft moss-covered glades. Here are noble oak trees, the production of a favourable and deep soil, so unlike the gnarled and twisted oaks that grow in stony places,

127

and above the tall oaks rises the noble Spanish chestnut, not the horse chestnut, but the tree of Salvator Rosa[29].

The tree of Salvator Rosa

A woodman making hurdles by the roadside under the shadow of a spreading chestnut tree takes charge of our machines while we enter one of the glades and wander deep into the recesses of the wood. Suddenly we come across a bed of the sweet lily of the valley close to a heathy spot and though we are too late for the bulk of the flowers sufficient remain to show how well the plant thrives here. We also notice many young plants of the Canterbury bell and we wonder if the name has been given to it from its profusion near the city of Canterbury. After a pleasant ramble in the wood, we continue our ride through a sweet-scented grove of pines; we leave Elbridge in a valley on our right and at a sign-post pointing 'to Thanet' we enter a delightful country road where we get a pretty view of Westbere, pass by a flourishing farmhouse with its grove of walnut and other trees and stop at the little village green in Stodmarsh. The church is an ancient simple structure of a type essentially Puritan, since it contains no decoration whatsoever except a few pieces of stained glass in the windows and 'Paris blue' on the walls. There is a wooden turret on the tower containing the two bells.

---

[29] Salvator Rosa (1615-1673) was an Italian Baroque painter, poet and printmaker, active in Naples, Rome and Florence.

Stodmarsh

The churchyard is an excellent example of the love for the sunny south side of a church in preference to the north. In the words of a poet:

"The rich and the poor all together
On the south of the church are sown,
To be raised in the same incorruption
When the trumpet at last is blown

On the north of a church lie buried
The dead of a hapless fame,
A cross and a wall for pity
But never a date nor name."[30]

Stodmarsh lies away from the beaten track of tourists and we have to make a long detour to reach Grove Ferry. After crossing the ferry we are again on the high road to Margate, and on our journey the quivering aspens, scarlet poppies, blossomed hawthorns, and white clover, remind us that we have charms around us which are denied to the dwellers in climes where eternal summer reigns and verdure maintains an unchangeable garb.

---

[30] Arthur Cleveland Coxe, Christian Ballads and Poems, Little Woodmere, The prayer-book pattern, pp114-121 (1849)

Modern directions for Ramble 5

From Margate's Turner Contemporary Art Gallery:

Travel along the seafront (Marine Drive) towards the clock tower

Turn right onto the A254 (Marine Terrace)

At the roundabout take the 3rd exit, onto the A28 Canterbury Rd, and follow this road to the roundabout at Birchington

Take the first exit onto the A28 Canterbury Rd

At the next roundabout take the 2nd exit (Canterbury Rd)

At Westbere turn left into Bushy Hill Rd

Continue along Bushy Hill Rd, into Westbere Lane to a 'T' junction

Turn left onto the A28 Canterbury Rd

Continue over the level crossing at Sturry, take the second right into High St

Take the first left into Church Lane to the church

Return along Church Lane and turn left into High St

Turn right at the 'T' junction into the A28 Sturry Hill

Take the first left into Fordwich Rd

Continue through Fordwich along King St and High St, then continue straight ahead, into Well Lane and on to a 'T' junction

Turn left into Stodmarsh Rd and through Stodmarsh to a 'T' junction

Turn right into Hollybush Lane

Take the first road on the left (no name) and continue to a 'T' junction

Turn left and continue to Grove Rd

Turn left into Grove Rd and continue to Grove Ferry

Cross over the railway line, up Grove Ferry Hill to a 'T' junction

Turn right onto the A28 Island Rd and continue to Margate

RAMBLE 6

(Maps 3, 4, 7, 9)

Distance approximately 60 miles

Margate

St Nicholas

Sarre

Upstreet

Westbere Butts

Sturry

Canterbury

St Dunstan's

Harbledown

Bigberry Wood

Dunkirk

Bosenden Wood

Boughton

Faversham

Preston

Boughton

Canterbury

Margate

On Margate sands

On a bright sunny morning at the end of the month of May I mount my iron steed for a sharp run out of Margate, my luggage being reduced to the smallest quantity, commensurate with comfort; it consisted of a small flask of lime juice with drinking cup attached, a case of sandwiches, a few nested pill boxes and my ordnance map of East Kent, all securely packed in a tiny bag.

To me, who have been used in earlier years to ramble over the wild upland where:

> *"The mill streams*
> *Which turn the clappers of the world*
> *Arise in solitary places,"[31]*

it is one of the freshest delights of returning summer to renew my acquaintances with the hills, to stand on a summit and look down upon 'a land of brooks and waters, a land of woods and giant trees, of leafy lanes, and park girt mansions', or to follow the tiny stream to its source.

> *"I see the rivers in their infant beds,*
> *Deep, deep, I hear them labouring to get free."[32]*

---

[31] Sir Arthur Helps (1813–1875)

And the object I have in view at starting on my ramble is to enjoy this delight with little fatigue.

The Parade, Margate 1890

At 7.45 I am riding along the Marine Parade towards Canterbury. The road is good, almost clear of vehicles and the little breeze blows cool from the east; so it occurs to me to attempt to reach Canterbury by nine o'clock. I ride steadily on without incident for mile after mile, the monotony being broken as I approach St Nicholas by a hare coming leisurely down the hill to meet me. At about a distance of fifty yards it suddenly stops, contemplates my machine and then races back in front of me for nearly a mile. I reach Sarre at 8.20 and here at the junction of the two roads, a butcher from Ramsgate with a fast trotting horse challenges me to keep up with him and gaily sets the pace. On the level road I gain upon him, but up the hill to Upstreet he gets well in front and looks back at me with triumph. The good hard and nearly level road is now in my favour and as we approach Westbere Butts the butcher begins to raise his whip and at the descent of Stain's Hill I am able to leave him behind so far that I get across the railway at Sturry as the porter closes the gate for a fast train to pass and the butcher is obliged to wait.

---

[32] James Thomson, The Seasons, Autumn

Victorian commercial horse and cart

At the Swan I take a short cut to the mill, and then keep steadily on past the pumping station, and the barracks, and arrive at the post-office in High street at two minutes past nine. Alas, the misfortune which stopped my pace maker at Sturry lost me those two minutes.

The Swan, Canterbury

I continue my route along High street, under the picturesque West Gate, through St Dunstan's and dismount at the steep ascent approaching the village of

134

Harbledown, from here I am at the commencement of what one of my cycling friends designates the 'mountains' beyond Canterbury.

To avoid the city centre and the pedestrianised High Street, consider taking this alternative route around Canterbury:

At the third roundabout after leaving Sturry, take the 3rd exit into Kingsmead Road. At the second roundabout, take the 1st exit into St Stephen's Road. At the second roundabout, close to the 'picturesque' West Gate, take the 2nd exit (i.e. turn right) and continue on to St Dunstan's.

St Dunstan's Street, Canterbury

With hills in front of me, I stop to rest and enjoy the view of Canterbury Cathedral. This is the view which pilgrims from London first obtain, and is, to my mind, the finest view of that beautiful edifice obtainable and is from a point due west.

In the village of Harbledown I stop to look at a pear tree, an old acquaintance, for in one of my journeys from London to Margate by road in the autumn there were on it large almost ripe pears, a second crop of tiny hard pears, and a third crop of blossom. Further on I make enquiries concerning the old Pilgrim Chapel and am told I have passed it, which I much regret, since it is said to be an interesting building.

Harbledown

Pilgrim's Hospital, Harbledown
This is also known as St Nicholas's Hospital.

The Black Prince's Well
This is sited at Harbledown, in the grounds of St Nicholas's Hospital.

A road on my left leads to Bigberry Wood, where there is an ancient British camp[33]. My experience of British camps is that, to the casual observer, they are merely banks of earth and when situated in woods are generally inaccessible, so I proceed on my journey. The road becomes steeper and steeper as I get further away from Canterbury and my pace is a slow one. Now I am at a spot where an Isle of Thanet smuggler outwitted the first of Russell's rural policemen he met with. The smuggler I speak of was of the bold kind and, as occasion offered, was in the habit of taking smuggled tobacco to London direct by road. His plan was to place the tobacco at the bottom of his cart, then cover it with one or more trusses of sweet smelling clover, and complete his load with light articles of furniture. He was slowly making his way up the hill, when he saw a policeman coming towards him. Without a moment's hesitation he pulled up at the side of the road, waited until the policeman reached him and then politely asked him to help push up the hill, which the policeman did, little suspecting he was aiding and abetting a smuggler. Though successful on this occasion our smuggler admits that the rural police eventually stopped the trade. I reach the top of the hill and at the Ville of Dunkirk leave my machine at a roadside inn.

---

[33] Iron Age hill fort

The Red Lion Inn, Dunkirk

Dunkirk Church, Boughton Hill

On such a morning as this, at the end of May, in the first year of Her Majesty's reign[34], there occurred at this place the tragedy of Bosenden Wood. The scene as I see it this morning seems of all others the most ill-suited for such a tragedy. No district can present a more thoroughly English character of quiet beauty. The village of Boughton-Under-Blean lies at the bottom of the hill. Herne Hill is away to the north, Goodnestone, Graveney and Selling are villages at short distances apart. Broad meadows, rich corn and clover fields, hedges bursting into blossom, scattered cottages with pretty gardens and farm houses surrounded with (and this is the most striking feature of the scene), orchards of apples and cherry trees,

---

[34] Queen Victoria: the battle was in 1838

covered with pink and white blossoms are all around. From the top of the hill there is an extensive open panorama. On the north is the sea with Faversham, Whitstable and Herne Bay at short distances; further away to the east are the towers of Reculvers and glimpses can be had of the Isle of Thanet. On the south, Shottenden Mill, situated in Stockbury Wood, in the centre of another British camp, is a conspicuous object. (Perry Wood, close by Shottenden, contains a third British camp, and probably most places in this neighbourhood having bury, perry, berry, and borough as a portion of the name were British settlements). Westward is the Isle of Sheppey with the wide estuary of the Swale and right across the valley of the Medway, as far as the eye can reach on the distant horizon, are Knockholt beaches. It is almost incredible that in such a district as this in the reign of the present Queen a madman should have been able to persuade people that he was the 'Messiah'.

At the entrance to the extensive woods I meet with an aged 'wood reeve', from whom I obtain a graphic account of the 'tragedy of Bosenden Wood'. With him I visit the oak trees at Mad Thom's corner; he relates the story of the music from heaven – a flute player concealed in a tree; points out where the constable Mears was shot; also the route taken by the military and the precise spot where the fanatic Courtney, followed by his ill-disciplined band, dared to attack the gallant soldiers of the 45th Regiment. He tells of the death of Lieutenant Bennett, of a volley fired by the soldiers when Courtney and eight others fell dead, besides several severely wounded, and of the flight of the rest of the misguided band. I listen to this story of fanaticism as to a romance, for near the place is a glade covered with wild hyacinths, a long stretch of blue, and a nightingale is pouring out its song in the thick under wood.

From here I ramble alone through the wood. The nightingale is everywhere, sometimes perched on a branch of a tall oak tree in full view, but more frequently hidden in the brushwood and occasionally in a bush by the side of a stream. The first stream I meet with is making its way east to Blean, Rushborne, Chislet and Reculvers; the second, only a few yards distant, is flowing north and goes into the sea at Swalecliffe. By the side of this clear stream I empty my case of sandwiches, the cool water and lime juice making a pleasant drink for my simple meal. Following the stream to its source, I find it rises in a damp, swampy place; and on my way I come across a flower I have never seen previously away from Covent Garden. Here it is in plenty, the plant resembling a lily in growth, with a simple white flower, while the scent is unmistakably 'garlic'.

I cross the road and ramble on until I come across a third stream, which is on the southern slope and is on its way to the River Swale; then I return almost to the first stream and yet a fourth gladdens my eyes as it flows down more quickly than the others, towards Harbledown and the River Stour above Canterbury. As I go through the wood I look sharply about me for flowers and insects. I fill my sandwich case with white hyacinths, lilies of the valley and small ferns, but my pill boxes are quite empty owing to the east wind, which causes lepidopteron of all kinds to take shelter out of sight.

From Dunkirk, where I pass the church built after the tragedy, I descend the steep hill, with feet at rest and brake applied, to the village of Boughton and,

139

having time to spare, decide to visit the church, which lies a mile to the left of the village, giving it the preference over Herne Hill, where Mad Thom lies buried without, it is said, any record, a mile to the right of Boughton.

The White Horse Inn with Boughton Church in the distance

A list of those killed in the Battle of Bosenden and buried in Herne Hill churchyard
John Nichols Thom is listed as John Tom. An Edward Wraight is listed as killed, but the name Edward Wraight was subsequently used by one of the survivors.

I apply at the rectory for the keys of the church and they are readily handed to me, with instructions how to use them. The church is an ancient building and might have been built by the architect of St Nicholas-at-Wade and St Peter's, Thanet. There are several good and interesting brasses. One of them, situated near and partly under the stove, illustrates at once the civilian dread style of epitaph and peculiar spelling (especially John for Joan) of a pre-Reformation period. The effigies of the lady and gentleman are remarkably good, and the epitaph runs thus:

"Pray for the soules of John Best, the elder, and John his wyf, the which John deceased the xx day of July, in the yere of our Lord MCCCCVIII. On whose soules jhn have mey."

Another brass is of a still more interesting character, as it gives a complete account of the person it commemorates. At the top is a shield and coat of arms, a deer and Prince of Wales feathers. The effigy is a big man in plate armour with a frill round his neck, and the epitaph describes him thus:

"I now that lye within this marble stone,
Was called Thomas Hawkins by my name,
My terme of life, an hundred years and one;
King Henry theigt I served which won me fame,
Who was to me a gratious Prince alwayes,
And made me well to spend my aged days.

My stature high, my bodye bigge and strong,
Excelling all that lived in mine age.
My nature spent, death would not tarry longe
To fetch the pledge which he had layed to gage
My fatall daye, if thou desire to know,
Behold the figures written here below:
16th March 1587."

Close by a very modest mural brass plate commemorates the wife of this doughty centenarian.

From Boughton Church a run of about twenty minutes takes me into the town of Faversham, where I get substantial refreshment. I merely look into the old church, which is undergoing its annual cleaning. It is noteworthy for possessing the bones of an English King, some curious fresco painting and a large number of brasses. The largest is of immense size, with elaborate canopies and marginal inscription, to the memory of a merchant adventurer, Henry Hatche, who died in 1538 and was evidently placed here during his wife's lifetime, for the date of her death has never been filled in. Another brass to Edward Blakwell reads, in place of the customary Anno Domini, *'Anno a Virgineo partu 1572'*.

141

Faversham Church

Whilst looking at these brasses a gentleman recommends me to see those in a neighbouring church 'Preston-next-Faversham', which I find in a better state of preservation than the Faversham ones. They consist of (1) Sir Valentine Baret (1422) in full armour, with helmet, sword and dagger and his dog at his feet; his wife is near him and is covered by a portion of the organ which, by the forethought of the Vicar, has been made movable. (2) Sir William Mareys, 1459, in armour, bareheaded and on each side a scroll bearing the words, 'Mercy Jhu;' and (3), Bennet Finch, 1612, in a richly embroidered dress. It is pleasing to see the care taken of these monuments and of the church itself.

Preston Street, Faversham

Preston-next-Faversham Church

After leaving Preston I overtake a cyclist who enquires the distance to Canterbury and the state of the road. I tell him we have one big hill to go up and soon afterwards Boughton Hill appears in front. My fellow cyclist's heart fails him, fatigued as he is with his journey from London and he exclaims, "Surely we have never to go up there?" When we reach Boughton we are besieged by a host of small boys whose cry is "Push you up, Sir." My companion accepts their offer and at once half-a-dozen harness themselves to his Coventry Rotary and we follow at our leisure.

An example of the Coventry Rotary from 1880

143

An easy run takes us to Canterbury. I bid him good-bye at the touring house, the Sir John Falstaff, and finish my return journey, satisfied that my ramble will give rest and solace to the brain. I feel with the poet Lowell that:

"The brain
That forages all climes to line the cells,
Will not distil the juices it has sucked,
Except for him who hath the secret learnt,
To mix his blood with sunshine and to take
The winds into his pulses"[35]

THE FALSTAFF INN AND WESTGATE, CANTERBURY.

Canterbury's West Gate with the Sir John Falstaff Hotel on the left

---

[35] James Russell Lowell, Under The Willows.
Original reads:
"...the brain
That forages all climes to line its cells,
Ranging both worlds on lightest wings of wish,
Will not distil the juices it has sucked
To the sweet substance of pellucid thought,
Except for him who hath the secret learned
To mix his blood with sunshine, and to take
The winds into his pulses."

144

Modern directions for Ramble 6

From Margate's Turner Contemporary Art Gallery:

Travel along the seafront (Marine Drive) towards the clock tower

Turn right onto the A254 (Marine Terrace)

At the roundabout take the 3rd exit, onto the A28 Canterbury Rd, and follow this road to the roundabout at Birchington, at which, take the first exit

Continue along the A28 , through Sturry and onto Sturry Rd

At the 3rd roundabout take the 3rd exit into Kingsmead Rd

At the roundabout take the 2nd exit

At the roundabout take the 1st exit, into St Stephen's Rd

At the roundabout take the first exit (North Lane)

At the roundabout take the 3rd exit onto the A290 (St Dunstan's St)

Continue over the railway crossing to a roundabout

Take the 1st exit into London Rd

At the next roundabout take the 3rd exit onto the A2050

Take the first left into Summer Hill

Continue through Harbledown into Church Hill

After ¼ mile turn right and then left and join the A2050

Take the first right into Roman Rd to Upper Harbledown

Bear left along Roman Rd and join the A2

After the service station, turn left onto the Canterbury Rd, through Dunkirk and Boughton

Turn left into Nine Ash Lane

At the 'T' junction turn left into Brenley Lane and on to Boughton Church

Return along Brenley Lane to the roundabout and take the 2nd exit onto the A2 Canterbury Rd

Take the first road on the right into the B2040 (Love Lane)

Bear left into Whitstable Rd, which becomes East Street

Turn right at the crossroads into Newton Rd (B2041) to the church

Return along Newton Rd, over the crossroads to a 'T' junction

Turn right into Station Rd, which becomes Forbes Rd

At the 'T' junction turn left into the Mall then right into Preston Lane to the church

Return along Preston Lane then take the first left into Preston Grove

At the 'T' junction turn left onto the A2 and return to Margate

RAMBLE 7

(Maps 3, 4, 5, 6, 7)

Distance approximately 70 miles

Margate

Sandwich

Statenborough

Eastry

Tilmanstone

Waldershare Park

Eythorne

Shepherdswell

Woolwich

Wickham Bushes

Swanton

Swingfield Minnis

Acrise

Elham Mill

Ottinge

Lyminge

Elham

Canterbury

Margate

Margate Jetty

The present ramble is one to which I look back with very great pleasure as one of the most enjoyable that I have had, in spite of the difficulties and mishaps which befell me, and which threatened to spoil my rambles entirely. Perhaps it is owing to having successfully overcome the difficulties that I retain such pleasant recollections of this particular excursion.

Soon after starting I notice a very slight clicking noise in my machine and I dismount, examine every part thoroughly and screw up all of the nuts with my spanner without discovering or removing the cause. When I get up full speed the click ceases until I reach my favourite mile on the Sandwich flats, the last mile but one before reaching Sandwich. Here I quicken my pace as usual, when suddenly one of the pedals drops off, the nut having broken in two. I work my way to Sandwich with one foot as best I can and am directed to a blacksmith, who very carefully replaces the broken nut and the only drawback I suffer from the breakage is a considerable loss of time. This is a greater evil than a non-cyclist might imagine, for the day is intensely hot and in order to complete my programme I am obliged to ride on during the heat of the day.

The Barbican and the old Bell Hotel, Sandwich
Notice the condition of the roads our cyclist had to contend with in 1886!
148

To negotiate the modern one-way system, turn left and around the Barbican into the High St. Follow the one-way system to a 'T' junction. Turn left into New St and follow this road over the level crossing to a roundabout. Take the first exit onto the Deal Rd and take the first turning on the right (Felderland Lane), to the 'T' junction at the A256 Sandwich Road. Turn left and then immediately right, signposted to Eastry.

After leaving Sandwich, I ride through the hamlet of Statenborough, where is an ancient camp, and pass through the picturesque village of Eastry – that puzzle to antiquaries and etymologists, for its name has been spelt at least a dozen different ways, as follows:– Estre, Estree, Estrei, Estrey, Estry, Estrye, Eastrie, Eastire, Easterye, Eastereye, Eastrye, and Eastry.

Lower Road, Eastry 1880

A new dual carriageway (A256 Dover Road) has been built to replace the old road. On leaving Eastry continue down Lower Street for about 500m, when the road becomes the old Dover road. At the approach to the modern roundabout, there is a cycle path (number 15) on the right. This cycle path follows the route of the old road to Dover, running alongside the new dual carriageway, passing Tilmanstone on the right. Continue to Waldershare Park. The old roadside inn ahead called 'The High and Dry', where our cyclist stopped for refreshments, is now a private residence and it appears that the route he took was through Waldershare Park, now a private road. Hence – turn right into Kennel Hill towards Eythorne and thence onto Shepherdswell.

The sun is intensely hot and reflects greater heat from the dusty chalk road as I mount the hill by Betshanger and proceed on past the village of Tilmanstone, a little way to my right. On such a day as this the cyclist suffers far more from thirst than from hunger and the appearance of a roadside inn close to Waldershare Park is sufficient today to cause me to dismount and refresh myself with a glass of soda and milk. Whilst I am talking to the landlord my attention is drawn to a very good· oil painting in his parlour – a picture with a history, for it has been in its present position for many years. The landlord says that it is supposed to be 300 years old and to be the portrait of Queen Mary. Should any lover of old paintings be passing by this way, he would do well to examine this picture, which resembles much the portraits of Sir Joshua Reynolds and may possibly be that of a court beauty of his time.

The High and Dry Inn, Waldershare
This was probably the inn visited by our cyclist, but is now a private residence.

From here I take a cross-country road with a view to find, if possible, the site of an ancient village mentioned in Ramble No. 2, but the road gradually grows less defined until it becomes a mere track across a ploughed field and I am obliged to push my machine in front of me. Outside this field I find another cross-country road and then take the first turning to the left. This road also gradually diminishes to a path across a field of barley. As it is my custom not to turn back unless compelled, I push forward, one wheel of my machine on the path and the other in the barley until I reach a plantation of pine trees, where the path widens sufficiently to allow me to ride comfortably, and at the end of the plantation I find another road of a very rough description.

While mounting the hill at Betshanger and in a chalky place near Waldershare Park, I have noticed on the banks adjoining the road that the smallest British butterfly, known as the Bedford Blue *(Lucoena Alsus)*, is on the wing and as I slowly emerge from the plantation into the narrow road, several specimens are visible at one time on the grassy side of the road. I dismount to capture a few specimens, but scarcely have I commenced operations when the rural postman, who also acts as deputy gamekeeper, appears on the scene and requests me not to disturb the pheasants, as there are nests close by. I can capture my small 'game' without leaving the roadside, so the postman's request meets with ready compliances. Little wonder that there are poachers in such an unprotected preserve as this!

The road improves as I approach the village of Eythorne and I cross the Chatham and Dover Railway at Shepherd's Well (Sibertswold) station.

Shepherd's Well

Then on through pleasant fields to the Hamlet of Woolwich[36] where I gladly dismount for a rest. The landlord of the village inn is also head gamekeeper of the extensive wood[37] which I have come to explore and I find no difficulty in obtaining permission from him to ramble through the wood, leaving my machine under his care.

---

[36] Now called Woolage Green

[37] The woods explored by our cyclist in 1886 are considerably smaller today

The Two Sawyers, Woolage Green

The wood is of large extent, and is situated on the highest ground in East Kent. From it the Isle of Thanet is conspicuous on the horizon, the cliffs of Ramsgate, Minster Mill and the towers of Reculvers being very distinct. In my ramble through the wood I notice numerous kinds of insects, but nothing especially local. I observe, however, several plants here that I never saw in such profusion before. One species of vetch attracts attention and another plant, the everlasting pea, which grows here in abundance, is quite new to me in its wild state. Outside the wood, I come upon a rough field with furze and coarse grass and here I discover the columbine growing wild. The only solution that I can think of for the presence here of both columbine and everlasting pea is that they are escaped garden flowers.

As a rule I always carefully choose the trunk of a tree or some piece of wood to rest upon in the country and avoid sitting on the grass for fear of future rheumatism, but today the heat causes me to relax my rule and no sooner do I lie down under the shadow of a tree than I am fast asleep and it is four o'clock when I awake; two hours lost and that, too, at the best of the day for the lepidopterist.

Returning through the wood I pick up a beautiful specimen of the jay and carry away with me its handsome wings. After taking counsel with the gamekeeper concerning my best route, I return almost to Shepherd's Well and then join the great Dover road.

The modern A2 dual carriageway bisects many of the old country roads, but can be traversed by the following route:

From Woolage Green, head back towards Shepherdswell to a 'T' junction, at which, turn right into Coxhill Road. Turn left onto the new A2 road, to a set of traffic lights. Turn right into Lydden Hill and take the first turning on the right, sign posted for Wickham Bushes. After about a mile, at the end of the public road, a public path takes you to a 'large farmhouse at Swanton'. Bear left at this farm and continue to the 'T' junction. Turn right into Swanton Lane and continue on to St John's Commandery, about a mile along on the left.

The first milestone I come to records 65 miles to London and a little nearer Dover. I turn off to the right to Wickham Bushes. Soon I come to a gate, and am told my way lies across the fields without a track of any kind. In addition to the ordinary roughness of these fields, there are several horses grazing therein and their hoofs in wet weather have made the field quite unrideable. After more than a mile of trudging across the fields I reach a large farmhouse at Swanton, where my machine causes much curiosity, since it is the first which has arrived there by that route, and the worthy farmer offers me his kind hospitality.

From here there is a 'hard' road, so called in this district to distinguish it from a field road and I try in some measure to make up for lost time. This district has a very pleasant primitive appearance, cattle being led along the roads to graze and many of the farms seem to be small, so that the work on them is done by the farmer and their families and the scenery is almost 'Flemish' in character. As I pass along, some of the houses are very quaint and at St John's is a curious old house which I fancy may have belonged to the Templars, but no one on the spot can give me any information. I leave Swingfield on my left, the church tower being visible, and descend by a steep but good road to Swingfield Minnis, Minnis in this part of Kent being synonymous with Common.

St John's Commandery

A corresponding ascent necessitates a walk up to Acrise, which appears as I pass by to consist of a few cottages, a shop and a blacksmith's forge, outside a park and mansion.

Acryse Rectory.

Acrise Rectory

Another steep descent skirting Acrise Park, another hill and a level run of a mile and I reach Elham Mill.

Elham Mill, circa 1900

At a cottage close by, I make enquiries as to the relative advantages of Elham and Lyminge with regard to hotel accommodation for the night and I am recommended to Elham, where there are three inns, while at Lyminge there is only one. I am directed to Elham by a field track, but having still a vivid recollection of the field track to Swanton, I decide to go to Lyminge.

Down an almost unrideable stony lane for half a mile, then over a bridge on the new railway covered with large flints and perfectly unrideable, into the valley of the Little Stour, now near its source. I proceed until I reach the main road at Ottinge, the sign post recording Lyminge one mile. After my late experience of stony roads and field tracks, the good road is pleasant and in a few minutes I enter the charming village of Lyminge. One of the first cottages is a grand specimen of a 14th or 15th century dwelling house, the black oak beams being very striking in contrast with the white washed plaster of the walls. I make my way to the little square bounded on one side by the churchyard and on another by the village inn, and at the inn the simple fact of my having come from Margate gains for me a hearty welcome and a bed, since the landlord's heart is at Margate and he has just had word from his wife, staying there for the benefit of her health, how much good the air of Margate is doing her.

The current Coach and Horses, Lyminge
This was built in 1888, replacing the original village inn in which our cyclist stayed in 1886.

Old well at Lyminge

After a hurried wash I visit the church close by. Canon Jenkins is at home, and under his guidance I examine the chief points of interest. In my numerous rambles I have seen many interesting old churches, but I must give the palm to Lyminge Church for its almost superabundance of historical associations. The vicar has endeavoured to restore the church to its early condition, and by removing the plaster from the walls of the interior, he has laid open to view various kinds of curious masonry. The lower part of the church was probably built by Lanfrase, in the eleventh century and his chancel is on a level with the nave.

There is some good herring bone masonry, probably done by a left-handed mason, also long and short work and specimens of later architecture. Outside the church are the foundations of the ancient Bastion, the Church of St Ethelburga, popularly known as Eadburg, and I look into the cemented tomb which held her remains until they were removed to Canterbury. This older church dates probably from the seventh century, and may also, like Reculvers Church, be connected to the Romans, so that a church may have been here in the fourth or early in the fifth century. It grows nearly dark as we examine the curious stone of the Bastion and the Roman concrete, which is hard as stone itself and we wonder how the old builders raised to their present height in the church tower the immense blocks of stone to be seen there.

St Mary and St Ethelburga, Lyminge

The day ends with supper at the inn and a pleasant hour spent in conversation with some engineers of the new railway who are superintending the boring of a tunnel near by. They are eloquent concerning Mount Canis, Severn and other noted tunnels, and explain that a special boring machine is necessary for chalk, the machines used at the two famous tunnels I have named having both failed here. They are on night duty and invite me to see their machine at work, but having had a hard day, with the prospect of another equally hard one to get back to Margate, I reluctantly decline.

Next morning I feel no trace of the previous day's fatigue and after breakfast I start on foot for Paddlesworth, a little hamlet with the smallest church in Kent, some three miles off.

Paddlesworth Church

The road is very hilly and when I get out into the open country my lepidopterist and botanical pursuits prevent my ever reaching Paddlesworth. There are few people in this quiet retired spot and the conversation of two young ladies as I pass them reveals at once their pursuit. The remark, "Neither a bee nor yet a butterfly," as one of them holds up a flower, proves that they are collecting orchids and not insects.

When I arrive at the top of the hill which has its slope to the south, I have reached the point which I had mapped out previously to starting on this my ramble, and as the dew is not yet quite dried up in shady places, I sit down on a stile and contemplate the extensive view. Over Folkestone is a mist, probably a sea fog; beneath me is the white chalk embankment of the new railway, next a circular hill with a tower on top and at the horizon, the sea.

The hill is covered with short grass and the tiny rock rose, *helianthemum vu'gare*, is plentiful on the slope. The object of my search are two insects known as Green Foresters – *Ino Geryon* and *Globularise*. The former when seen on the wing in the sunshine is merely a bright bronze speck, overlooked by everybody except the entomologist and the eye requires training to its peculiar flight. At first I discovered a specimen at long intervals only, but with experience, the difficulty of finding them diminished. The larger *Globularise* was easily seen, but much less plentiful. The capture of two species I had never seen before alive quite satisfied me for today. The common insects on the hill were Burnet Moths by hundreds, Small Blues and a few Clouded Bluffs, *E. Russula*.

Here I discover the orchids the young ladies were in search of. The bee orchid, which I consider the very best imitation of an insect in the British flora, is plentiful and in beautiful condition and the curious, but less imitative, 'butterfly' orchid can also be obtained. Having arranged to dine at 2 pm, I return to Lyminge by way of Eachend Hill where the new railway is being made and watch for some little time the operation of tipping chalk over the embankment.

Our cyclist explores this beautiful countryside on foot. If walking is not on the agenda, the following route will offer a similar experience:

From Station Road head out of Lyminge towards Postling. Passing Mayfield Road on the right and Everest Court on the left, take a turning on the left called Greenbanks. Passing the car park take the first turning on the right. Passing the bungalows on the left, continue for approx 400m. to a fork in the road (just before the signpost for Red House Farm). Take the right fork (signposted) along a rough track, which can become rather muddy after rainfall but improves near the end. The track passes the golf course on the right and ends at Teddars Leas Road.

The rough track after rainfall

Turn right towards Etchinghill. The views here across a hilly landscape, mentioned by our cyclist, are well worth the visit. On reaching Etchinghill turn into Westfield Lane (a dead end road). At the end of this road one is as close to Each End Hill (which our cyclist says he 'returns to Lyminge by way of') as is possible by bicycle and one is rewarded with more wonderful views. Being on foot, our cyclist would have been able to access parts of the long distance footpaths such as the Elham Valley Way or the North Downs Way, which criss-cross the countryside here. From this point, either head directly back to Lyminge and hence to Margate, or return to Etchinghill and Teddars Leas Rd, head for Paddlesworth and refer to the route text at the end of this Ramble for directions.

After dinner I start homeward, leaving the majority of the inhabitants of Lyminge watching a tennis match between two local teams, in which they appear to take great interest. At first I jog along quietly on account of the heat of the sun, stop at Elham a little while and try to get inside the church to see the library, but cannot find the man who keeps the keys.

159

Elham Square, circa 1900
The houses in front of the church no longer exist.

The road is good, except at a new bridge over the railway, which I am told was just opened, my vehicle being the first to cross and workmen offering to carry it over. The valley of the Little Stour, down which the road runs, is very picturesque, with woods on one side and wooded downs on the other, and as the afternoon progresses my ride becomes more enjoyable.

I pass Dorringstone Church and village at a rapid rate down a hill and unfortunately miss Kingstone on my left hand, that being a place I wish to visit. I join the Dover road at Barham Downs and ride thence to Canterbury without stopping. I get a late tea at Baker's and finish my journey without further incident.

Baker's Hotel, Canterbury

Modern directions for Ramble 7

From Margate's Turner Contemporary Art Gallery:

When starting this ramble one needs to travel up Margate's High Street from the harbour area. Parts of the High Street have been pedestrianised during certain times of the day, necessitating a dismount. On reaching St John's Church, at the end of the High Street, keep to the right of the church and enter the one-way system (A255) for about 100m to some crossroads. Bear right onto the Ramsgate Rd (A254, under the railway bridge (once the site of East Margate Station) and on to the traffic lights

Continue along the A254 Ramsgate Rd to a roundabout at Westwood Cross. Take the 3rd exit, onto the A256 (Haine Rd)

Continue along the A256, across 4 roundabouts to a double roundabout

Take the 1st exit at the 1st roundabout and the 2nd exit at the next, into the A256 Sandwich Rd and past the Viking Ship and Pegwell Bay Nature Reserve

At the next roundabout take the 1st exit

At the next roundabout take the 2nd exit, towards Sandwich

At the next roundabout take the 1st exit, along the Ramsgate Rd

At the next roundabout take the 1st exit

At the next (small) roundabout, take the 2nd exit and on to the bridge into Sandwich

Follow the one-way system, around the Barbican into the High St, to a 'T' junction

Turn left into New St, and travel over the level crossing to a roundabout. Take the first exit onto the Deal Rd (A258)

Take the first turning on the right into Felderland Lane

At the staggered junction, turn left then immediately right into Sandwich Rd and on through Eastry

Join the cycle path on the right, about 50m before the roundabout, and continue towards Waldershare passing Tilmanstone, signposted on the right

At Waldershare turn right into Kennel Hill, towards Eythorne

At the roundabout take the 1st exit, into Coldred Rd

At the crossroads turn right into Long Lane

At the crossroads turn left into Eythorne Rd

At Shepherdswell, cross the railway line and take the first right, into Westcourt Lane to Woolage Green (previously known as Woolwich)

Return to Shepherdswell and turn right into Coxhill Rd

At the 'T' junction turn left onto the A2 Dover Rd

At the traffic lights turn right into Lydden Hill

After about ½ mile turn right (no road name) towards Wickham Bushes

Pass through a gate onto a footpath/bridleway and continue to a 'T' junction

Turn right into Swanton Lane and continue for about two miles to the crossroads at Swingfield Minnis, at which cross over the A260 Canterbury Rd into Hoad Rd

At the 'T' junction at Acrise, turn right (no road name) and follow the road round a left-hand bend and take the first road on the right, towards Ottinge

At the 'T' junction turn left onto the Canterbury Rd

Continue along Canterbury Rd through Lyminge into Station Rd, which becomes Canterbury Rd once again

DETOUR TO PADDLESWORTH:

Continue to Newbarn and bear left along the Canterbury Rd to Etchinghill

Turn left into Teddars Leas Rd and follow the road towards Paddlesworth

Follow the road round past Paddlesworth bearing left all the time to a 'T' junction

Turn right towards Shuttlesfield

At Shuttlesfield turn left to a 'T' junction at Mill Down Farm

Turn left at the junction to the next 'T' junction, near Ottinge

At the junction turn right into the Canterbury Rd

RETURN JOURNEY

Follow the Canterbury Rd through Elham, Wigmore, Breach, Barham, Kingston and Bridge all the way to Canterbury and follow the signs for Margate

RAMBLE 8

(Maps 3, 7, 8)

Distance approximately 50 miles

Margate

Dane Valley

Woodchurch

Acol

Sarre

Canterbury

St Lawrence

Nackington

Lower Hardres

Upper Hardres

Chartham

Thanington

Canterbury

Margate

Bathers' waiting room at Margate

It is the custom to look upon the good old town of Margate as altogether a modern erection, a mere fashionable seaside resort of the dwellers in the metropolis in the nineteenth century, and it is said that three hundred years ago it was a tiny fishing village containing about one hundred inhabitants. Before beginning my ramble, I will just touch upon this subject.

More than three hundred years ago, in the reign of Good Queen Bess, there lived a 'rambler' of the name of Lambarde, who published an account of his rambles in a book which is known as 'Lambarde's Perambulation of Kent', a book full of quaint, amusing and interesting information concerning the county of Kent, including the Isle of Thanet. Amongst other interesting items, he has published the particulars of an assessment made in the thirteenth year of Queen Elizabeth, 1570-1, for the payment of Kentish villes and boroughs to the crown of a tenth and fifteenth. The county is divided into hundreds and the first on the list is the hundred of Kingslowe, which consists of the Isle of 'Tenet'. Possibly the spelling of the hundred may be due to a printer's error, for it is usually spelt Ringslow or Ryngsloe. Since the grouping of the villes in this hundred is of importance and as it may be interesting to compare their valuation with that of the present day, I will insert a portion of the subsidy list. Each 'ville' is therein called a 'towne':

	£	s	d
The towne of Wood	4	7	8
The towne of Monkton	3	0	0
The towne of Mynster	15	0	0
The towne of S. Lawrence	17	13	4
The towne of S. Peter	15	17	0
The towne of S. John	23	12	0
The towne of S. Giles	0	15	0
The towne of S. Nicholas	10	7	0
The towne of All Sainctes	4	6	4
The towne of Byrchingstone	8	15	3
Sum of the Hundreth of Kingslowe	£103	13	7

One looks in vain down the list for the town of Margate, but in its place stands that of S. John and I may remark that whilst the hundred of Kingslowe was at that time the most valuable in Kent, being more than double that of any of the rest, with one or two exceptions, the town of Margate, then known as St John's, had the proud pre-eminence of having to pay the highest tax exacted from any ville or borough in the county, viz, the sum of £23 12s, whereas Maydestone was valued at £19 9s 2d., and Chetham at £8 10s only, a smaller sum than that paid by the villages of St Nicholas and Birchington.

I commence this ramble in the valley of the 'Dane' and possibly there may have been here a small fishing community living close to the sea. The name Dane carries our thoughts back at least one thousand years, to the period when:

> *"Those Danish louts, whom hunger starved at home,*
> *Like wolves pursuing prey around the world did roam."*[38]

And possibly the 'Danish Pyrats' of Lambarde landed in this valley. I ascend slowly out of the Dane by the Victoria road and as I approach the Church of St John, I notice several groups of old houses. Quite sufficient to show that probably this is the site of the old town of St John's, which must have been in a flourishing state three hundred years ago, for it is needless to remark that a mere handful of cottages, a dozen to a score, in which one hundred people might dwell, would never be rated at the large sum of £23. Probably there were then two divisions of the town, the larger portion next the church and a small hamlet by the sea.

My destination today is the village of Chartham, where I have arranged to meet some friends, who will travel by rail to the flower show there and having plenty of time I ride leisurely along, merely noting the aspect of the fields and hop gardens on this, a bright day in August. I pass Shottendane, Hengrove and at Woodchurch I ask myself 'Where is now the towne of Wood?' Then on through Acol to Mount Pleasant and the Ville of Sarre, formerly the towne of St Giles. Canterbury is reached by eleven o'clock and, as I am not due at Chartham until

---

[38] Michael Drayton

two pm, I take the opportunity to visit a few villages lying out of the beaten track of tourists.

High Street, Acol

With this object in view I proceed from the cattle market along the Old Dover road and I skirt the noted cricket ground of St Lawrence, where a short time previously I had seen the Kentish cricketers defeat crack teams of Australians and Yorkshiremen. Then the cricket field was crowded with spectators and gay with bunting, but now not a solitary individual can be seen.

Dover Road cattle market, Canterbury, circa 1900

The road is excellent past Nackington House and street, and half a mile further on I notice a little church away on my left hand, apparently standing alone in the field. I turn down a road leading to it and find it is on the outskirts of the village of Nackington. Once more I have to mention the care bestowed on village churches in Kent and this church of Nackington, though small in size, lacks nothing that is necessary for public worship. In its vaults lie buried several members of the Sondes family and their monuments on the walls are an interesting feature.

Nackington House

Nackington Church

167

The next village I arrive at is Lower Hardres, where the road becomes more hilly. The church is a handsome building of recent date and possesses little interest for the antiquarian, but provides a greater degree of comfort for the worshippers than many older edifices. Here I am directed to the next village, known as Upper Hardres and I am told that the church there is very ancient and contains some curious brasses. I am also considerately informed how to obtain the keys of the church and this information saves me from loss of time. In places the road is rough and stony, a drawback in great measure compensated for by the extensive views obtainable on the little hills. As I reach Upper Hardres I wonder whence the worshippers come to the old church, for the village appears to consist of a farmhouse and a few cottages only. I continue my ride to the parsonage, half a mile further on, where I get the keys and return to the church. I notice on my way that large farms have recently been for sale in this immediate neighbourhood and I am told it is difficult to get a purchaser at reasonable terms.

The interior of the church tells its history very plainly. A wealthy family formerly resided here of the name of Hardres, inscriptions being left of them (effigies gone) dating from 1482 to 1579, and since then the church has decayed, so that it would now benefit from restoration. The inscription of 1579 contains the names of the children of Mabel Hardres, wife of Richard Hardres Esquire, as follows: 'Thomas! Thomas, Roger, John! Peter, Mary! Jane'. The mark! After the name indicates that they died before their mother. The special feature in the church is a brass to the memory of a former rector, whose effigy is represented in a kneeling position at the foot of a pillar, which supports the effigies of St Peter and St Paul. A scroll bearing an inscription winds round the pillar and the epitaph at the foot reads thus: *"Hic jacet magist Johes sturt quodui Rector hui ecclie qui obiit vi die February Adui MCCCCVXIII. Aie ppicciet ds. Ame."*[39]

Upper Hardres Church

---

[39] According to www.upperhardreschurch.co.uk/brasses.htm, the inscription reads: *"Hic jacet Magist Johes Strete quodm Rector hui ecclie qui obiit vi die Februarii A.Dni MCCCCV cui aie ppiciet Ds. Ame."* ("Here lies Master John Strete, formerly Rector of this Church, who died February 6th, A.D. 1405, on whose soul may God have mercy. Amen.")

After leaving the church it is necessary to go back to the parsonage with the keys, from hence I hurry to Canterbury the same way that I came[40] and after dinner ride leisurely to Chartham. My friends have arrived by train and we at once pay a visit to the flower show, after which we decide to make a tour of the village.

Chartham

The Artichoke Inn, Chartham

---

[40] To avoid travelling back to Canterbury an alternative route to Chartham can be obtained from www.victoriancyclist.com

Bedford House, Chartham

Under the heading Chartham, Lambarde, in his 'Perambulation of Kent', has a long chapter, but it contains nothing concerning the village itself, except that in the reign of Edward I, when the Pope claimed jurisdiction in England at the close of the thirteenth century:

"Onely Robert of Winchlesey (then Archbishop of Canterbury) refused to aide the King, or to reconcile himselfe, in so much that of very stomacke he discharged his familie, abandoned the Citie, and withdrew himselfe to this Towne, the whiche was first given to his priorie of Christes church by one Alfred, a noble man, about the yeere after Christ, 970: and from thence (as mine Author saith) he roade each Sunday and Holiday to the churches adjoining, and preached the woorde of God."

The noble church in which Robert of Winchlesey preached still remains and is one of the finest village churches in the district. Not many years ago it was restored and a magnificent roof was brought to light, having previously been hidden by a ceiling of lath and plaster. The chancel is beautifully ornamented, chiefly by the labours of the Vicar and his family, and the north transept contains one of the finest and most ancient effigies in brass to be found in England, that of

170

Sir Robert Septuans in chain armour, with his coat of arms, a winnowing fan or shield and epaulettes. From the crossing of his legs he had been in several Crusades and the date of the brass is fixed at 1306. We are so struck with its beauty that we set to work and make a rubbing and the result proves the truth of the adage 'A thing of beauty is a joy for ever'. Close by is an effigy of later date, which shows the rapid decadence in the art of working in brass. Whilst the effigy of 'Septuans' is of more than life-size, well-proportioned, with handsome features and is exquisitely engraved, that of 'Jane Lucas' is diminutive, uncouth in form and roughly finished, but its epitaph is worthy of record from the curious spelling of some of the words:

> *"Off youre charyte te pray for the soule of Jane Lucas*
> *dowtt of jewyl clefforbt squyre sche desest the XI.*
> *day of Junius in the yere of owur lord God*
> *MVCXXX on hoss soule jhs haue marsec."*

Unfortunately 'Septuans' has no inscription and the greater portion of the dog on which his feet rest has been broken away. There are three other brasses, all of which have, like Septuans, the Christian name of Robert, viz, Rev. Robert London, 1416, Rev. Robert Arthur, 1454 and Rev. Robert Sheffield, 1506.

Chartham Church

171

On the departure of my friends by the train I mount my machine and start homewards. The shadows thrown by the setting sun are lengthening fast as I approach the little village of Thanington, less than two miles from Chartham. I dismount at the gate of the churchyard for this spot claims to be the scene of that beautiful idyll, 'Grey's Elegy written in a country churchyard'. A similar claim being made on behalf of Stoke Poges:

> *"Beneath these rugged elms, that yew trees shade*
> *Where heaves the turf in many a mouldering heap*
> *Each in his narrow cell forever laid,*
> *The rude forefathers of the hamlet sleep."*

Under the yew tree's shade a seat has been placed and as I sit here, the landscape and other allusions of the elegy can be discerned:

> *"The lowing herd wind slowly o'er the lea,*
> *The ploughman homeward plods his weary way*
> *And drowsy tinklings lull the distant folds."*

The place is suitable for reflection and this venerable yew tree might also have inspired Tennyson, when he wrote those beautiful lines in his 'In memoriam':

> *"Old yew which grasped at the stones*
> *That name the underlying dead*
> *Thy fibres net the dreamless head*
> *Thy roots are wrapped about the bones.*
>
> *The seasons bring the flower again*
> *And bring the fledglings to the flock*
> *And in the dusk of there the clock*
> *Beats out the little lives of men*
>
> *Oh not for thee the glow, the bloom*
> *Who changest not in any gale*
> *Nor branding summer suns avail*
> *To touch thy thousand years of gloom"*

St Nicholas Church, Thanington

I remount my machine and approaching the city of Canterbury, I am still further reminded of Grey's elegy as "The curfew tolls the knoll of parting day" from the Cathedral tower. I light my lamps before entering the city and for the rest of my journey:

"The air is hush'd save where the weak-eyed bat
With short shrill shriek flits by on leathern wing,
Or where the beetle winds
His small but sullen horn"[41]

---

[41] William Collins, Ode To Evening

Modern directions for Ramble 8

From Margate's Turner Contemporary Art Gallery:

Turn left into Market St

At the 'T' junction turn left into Hawley St

At the crossroads turn right into King St

Continue along King St into Dane Rd then turn right at the crossroads into Victoria Rd, all the way to the A254 Ramsgate Rd

At the traffic lights turn right into the B2052 (College Rd)

At the next set of traffic lights go straight across into Shottendane Rd

Continue along Shottendane Rd to a 'T' junction

Turn right then immediately left into Margate Hill

At the next 'T' junction, in Acol, turn left into The Street (B2048) which becomes Minster Rd

At the roundabout take the 2nd exit

At the next roundabout, take the 3rd exit onto the A299 Canterbury Rd West

After about 150m take the road on the left (the original road, running parallel to the modern dual carriageway)

At the 'T' junction turn right to the roundabout and take the 1st exit (A253)

At the Sarre roundabout take the 1st exit onto the A28 Island Rd

Follow the ring road around Canterbury and take the B2068 Old Dover Rd past St Lawrence cricket ground

Turn right into the B2068 Nackington Rd

After about 1½ miles cross over the A2 and turn left into Church Lane, to Nackington

Return to the B2068 Nackington Rd and turn left

Take the 2nd turning on the left, Hardres Court Rd, through Lower Hardres to Upper Hardres

Return from Upper Hardres to the B2068 and turn left then right, into Chartham Downs Rd

Continue for about 3½ miles and turn right into Cockering Rd. At the roundabout take the 1st exit (Cockering Rd)

Turn left into Rattington St, and continue through Chartham, along Station Rd and over the railway to a 'T' junction

Turn right onto the A28 Ashford Rd, and travel through Thanington and then Wincheap, onto the Canterbury ring road and head for Margate

RAMBLE 9

(Maps 3, 8, 7, 10)

Distance approximately 80 miles

Margate

Sarre

Upstreet

Sturry

Canterbury

Wincheap

Thanington

Chartham

Godmersham

Buckwell

Wye

Brabourne

The Downs

Weald of Kent

Brooke

Olantigh Park

Canterbury

Margate

Bathing Machines on Margate beach

One of the greatest difficulties in the way of making the account of my rambles interesting is that there are only two roads by which I can get out of the Isle of Thanet; one of these roads goes through the Ville of Sarre and the second passes over the drawbridge across the River Stour at Sandwich. Once outside the island, rambles can be taken in every direction, but the cyclist, as a rule, prefers to keep to the main roads.

Today I have decided upon a long ride and start early in order to get the greater portion of the journey completed before the sun gets too hot. We are approaching the close of the month of August, but we are not yet free from sultry heat, when it is advisable for the cyclist who journeys for pleasure to rest awhile. The appearance of the sky as I leave Margate portends heat and a dense mist nearly blots out the sea from view. When I reach Sarre at seven o'clock, I find the white mist still more dense across the marshes, and as I ride along the level, the trees on each side present a weird appearance as they successively come into view.

Through Upstreet and Sturry I am debarred from enjoyment of the landscape, from watching for glimpses of the River Stour and from obtaining a distant view of the noble Cathedral of Canterbury. How different is the scene when the sun lights up the whole valley.

To avoid the city centre and the pedestrianised High Street, consider taking this alternative route around Canterbury:

At the third roundabout after leaving Sturry, take the 3ʳᵈ exit into Kingsmead Road. At the second roundabout, take the 1ˢᵗ exit into St Stephen's Road. At the second roundabout, take the first exit, through the West Gate. Follow the road to the next roundabout and take the first exit. At the next roundabout, take the third exit, through Wincheap.

The Black Mill on the River Stour, Sturry

At Canterbury I turn down by the Rose Hotel and make my way as best I can to Wincheap, then take the main road to Ashford through the village of Thanington.

The Rose Hotel, Canterbury

The mist is becoming less dense, yet at Chartham I can detect no trace of the immense asylum on the hill and Chilham Church on my right hand is invisible from the same cause:

"The distant spire across the vale,
Those floating vapours shroud,
Scarce are the neighbouring poplars seen,
Pale, shadowed in the cloud"[42]

St Augustine's Psychiatric Hospital (Asylum) 1875-1993, Chartham
The hospital was closed in 1993 and in 1997 development of the site for housing began. A few of the hospital buildings, including the administration block, the water tower, and the chapel, were retained but the rest were demolished. Although Canterbury City Council suggested that "a change of name would help in creating a new sense of identity", the site is known as St Augustine's Estate.

At the little village of Godmersham I pass close by the picturesque church, with its trim, well-kept churchyard. Reluctantly I postpone making acquaintance with its interior, for I have still several miles to ride before reaching my destination.

---

[42] Robert Southey, The Morning Mist

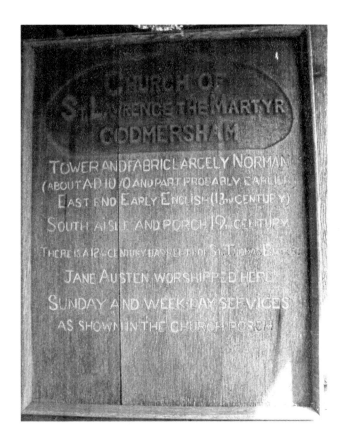

Jane Austen's connection to Godmersham Church recorded in the church grounds

Godmersham Park House

This was once the residence of Jane Austen's brother Edward. Today, the house is privately owned and used as a training and study centre.

Two miles further on, at a little place called Buckwell, I make my first stoppage, to have a chat with a Margate resident, who stops me as I am hurrying past, and from him I get some information concerning my route.

My next stoppage is at the village of Wye for a late breakfast, after which I pay a visit to the church, which I find open. There is a notice at the entrance, of an organ recital to be given later in the day by the vicar of Folkestone, and I get the benefit of a rehearsal whilst I examine the church. Perhaps owing to its position in the valley of the Stour, in a break in the continuity of the North Downs, this church appears to be especially liable to injury from lightning and has been struck several times with curious effects. The interior has little or no ornamentation, being a good specimen of the type known as evangelical. There are some brasses in the nave, much worn by the constant tramping of feet of the congregation over them.

Church Street Wye, with its church in the background

The Crown in the hillside just outside Wye
This was carved in the chalk by students in 1902, to commemorate the coronation of Edward VII.

180

The mist still obscures the hills and as the forenoon advances I begin to fear that one of the objects of my journey, a visit to Wye Downs in search of lepidoptera, will be in vain. I decide in the meanwhile to search for 'archaeological' treasures. As soon as I leave Wye I enter upon a district which has been immortalised by the literary genius of Lord Brabourne (Knatchbull Hugessen[43]), for I am not ashamed to own that his fairy tales have given me immense delight – some of them I can read over and over again. I enquire my way to the village of Brabourne and have a choice of two roads, an upper and a lower, the latter being recommended as the best for my machine.

The little village of Brooke, nestling under the Downs with its old Norman church, lies enshrouded in mist on my left hand and Hinxbill is on my right, with Willesborough Church, famous for its ancient memorial windows, still further on the right. These are all places rendered familiar by the before-mentioned fairy tales. The road winds about in a most unaccountable fashion, so that, possibly through an error on my part, I find myself on the upper road, skirting the Downs, instead of on the lower, which I had chosen to follow.

The bank on one side of the road is carpeted with flowers and only sunshine is requisite for it to be swarming with insect life. The readers of 'Queer Folk' can here recognise the hollow mentioned in the 'Warlock of Coombe' and I notice several places which might well serve for his residence at the present time.

The road passes through a number of fields with gates to be opened and closed and I should scarcely be surprised to discover myself in the land of the 'pig-faced lady', when my arrival at the village of Brabourne dissolves all idea of fairy land, as the school children hurry out for their forenoon recess with unmistakeably human voices and features.

The Five Bells Inn at Brabourne

---

[43] Edward Knatchbull-Hugessen, 1st Baron Brabourne, (1829-1893) was a British Liberal politician. Hugessen wrote fairy-tales for his children some of which are well known: Stories for My Children (1869), Crackers for Christmas (1870), Moonshine (1871), Tales at Tea Time (1872), Queer Folk (1874) and Friends and Foes from Fairyland (1886)

Old buildings near the church at Brabourne

Brabourne Church contains much of interest for the archaeologists and antiquarians and has been carefully restored so that the interior is in a perfect state of preservation. The present vicar kindly opens the doors for me and then leaves me to examine the church at my leisure, after having pointed out the objects of greatest interest. Sir Gilbert Scott considered that this church was as good and admirable a specimen of the late Norman work as could be found in the kingdom. The chancel is the most perfect portion. It is pure Norman and every block of the original work is a picture in its skilled workmanship; it is difficult to understand what tools or sleight of hand enabled those ancient artificers to produce such exquisite work, far superior to that of modern days.

Brabourne Church

The carving of the capitals on the chancel arch is admirable, the lines being apparently as sharp and well defined as when first cut some 700 years ago. The priest's entrance on the north is one of the simplest doors in the world, but one of the most picturesque and artistic and in one of the cleaned windows, there is, what is rarely met with, some of the original stained glass of the Norman period. Besides the architectural features of the church, its monuments deserve careful inspection.

The first and most important to my mind is the 'heart shrine', the only one I have seen. Its history is a touching one. It belonged to the family of Balliol, who were claimants to the throne of Scotland and one of them, who was the founder of Balliol College, Oxford, was the Lord of Galloway. At his death in the year 1269, his devoted wife had his heart embalmed and placed in a case of ivory and silver, which was carried about wherever she went and at meals placed on his accustomed seat. In his memory she founded a beautiful abbey, which she named Dulcecor – *dulce,* sweet, and *cor,* heart – and directed that she should be buried there and her husband's heart beside her. This was done, but in the troublesome times which followed, the Balliols fled from Scotland and it is supposed that the heart was brought here and enshrined[44]. The ruins of Dulcecor Abbey, near Dumfries, are of the same style of architecture as the heart shrine here and both are beautiful examples of the early English style.

The 'Heart Shrine' in Brabourne Church

---

[44] The heart is supposedly that of John de Baliol. After being buried alongside his wife according to her wishes, it was eventually brought to this little church at Brabourne, probably by one of her sons, John Baliol le Scott, who was elected King of Scotland in 1292. John was subsequently defeated and exiled by Edward I, and it is at this time the heart probably arrived at Brabourne Church. John passed on custody of the heart to his brothers, Alexander Baliol, who was Lord of Chilham Castle, and Sir William Baliol le Scott, the original ancestor of the Scotts of Scott Hall. In the same way in which the ancestral home has disappeared with the passing of the years so, it appears, has the heart and its casket.
(Source: www.kentresources.co.uk/brabourne.htm)
According to www.kentchurches.info, it is uncertain whose heart was buried here, but it dates from about 1296 and may be associated with the de Valence family.
(Source: www.kentchurches.info/church.asp?p=Brabourne)

Another remarkable monument is placed under the chancel window, at the east end of the church, and from its peculiar situation resembles altar and reredos combined. The stone of which it is made is known as Bethersden marble and the whole monument is beautifully ornamented. The text of the scripture inscribed upon it shows that it was probably erected towards the close of the sixteenth century, and the arms are those of the Scotts, descendents of the Balliols.

On the north side of the chancel is an earlier monument belonging to the same family and commemorating Sir John Scott, who was Warden of the Cinque Ports in the reign of Edward IV. He died in 1485 and left behind him a very curious book containing an account of his expenses "fro the XVIII day of Aur ell the III yere of ye King" (Edward IV, A.D. 1464).

The following are a few extracts therefrom:

fiyrst Brought to London in a Bagge of Gold,	IIj xx li	[£181]
It Bought in an our Bagge	IIj iis	[£150 2s]
It for a payre of hosy'n & 10 payre of Sokks	iijs iiijd	[3s 4d]
It paid to the Sadeliare	xls	[40s]
It paid to ye Sadeliars man of Gyft	Xijd	[12d]
It paid to John Southilete for a blak ambelying Gyldyng	xls	[40s]
It to my Corueser	vjs viij d	[6s 8d]
It for hyryng of iii Hakenneyys	x s	[10s]
It paid in full payme't for the furre and furryng of my wife's govne	lv s	[55s]
It paid for my lent stuffe of salt fyssh the last yere passed	xiijs iiijd	[13s 4d]
It geve to the surgun fore helyng of my legge	iijs iiijd	[3s 4d]

Altogether the bodies of about seventeen generations of 'Scotts' lie buried in the church and in addition to the stone monuments there are, on the floor, four brasses in an excellent state of preservation.

No. I. Represents a knight in full armour, under a canopy with his feet resting on a Talbot[45] or dog; the description is gone, but it is supposed to represent Sir Wm Scott, who died in 1433.

No. II. Is the effigy of a lady, a striking feature being that she is represented with long flowing hair reaching to the knees. The inscription is also gone, but there is evidence in existence to show that the brass commemorates Lady Clifton, second wife of the above Sir Wm Scott

No. III. Bears a curious inscription, commencing with *"Of your Charite pray for the soule of Sir Wm Scott,"* date 1524 and ends with *"On whos sowle of your charite saye a Paternoster and an Ave."* This brass is a knight in full armour, but the whole appearance is much less graceful than the knight shown in No. I.

---

[45] A large breed of hunting dog, now extinct

No. IV. Represents Dame Elizabeth Pownynges, sister of the last mentioned Sir Wm Scott, who died in 1528. The engraving of this brass is exquisite, and as sharp and as clear as when fresh from the hands of the engraver.

The church stands in a beautiful situation, surrounded by trees with the vicarage adjoining, and the exterior is well worth examination. On returning the keys I pass by the tomb of the late vicar, close to the east end of the church, through whose instrumentality the church was restored to its present satisfactory condition and of whom it may be said:

> *"Rich he was in holy thought and work*
> *And thereto a right learned man"*[46]

I now prepare to pay a visit to the Downs and whilst wheeling my machine from beneath the shadow of the trees of the churchyard, I am accosted by a gentleman who, somewhat to my surprise, asks if I have come from Margate and then invites me to partake of his kind hospitalities. To him I am indebted for much interesting information concerning the church I have just visited. After a pleasant half hour spent in the fine building occupied by my benevolent host, I remount my machine and go on my way rejoicing, for in the meantime the mist has entirely disappeared, the sun is shining his full strength and when I reach the edges of the Downs:

> *"Then do I see across the vale*
> *The village spire so white*
> *And the grey wood and meadow green*
> *Shall live again in light"*[47]

The flowery banks I passed on my way to Brabourne are now swarming with lepidoptera, several handsome specimens of Diurnal giving colour and gaiety to the scene. *Inachis Io* with its beautiful eyelike spots, *Atala* again with its brilliant red bands on a black background beautiful in its fresh tints and *Rhamni* looking like an orange coloured flower when seated on the scabious, all these lovely insects are common and are here flying leisurely about before they take to their winter quarters, perchance some ivy-covered church tower, where they will rest dormant until the warmth of spring brings them out to renew their gyrations after six months' hibernation. A few specimens of *Edure* come racing gaily along with the breeze, but it is evident this species is not as common this year as it is occasionally and *Hyale* is entirely absent. The little *Paleas* shine like a bright copper brooch, and fights for the possession of almost every flower with its companion *Alexis* arrayed in blue.

---

[46] Chaucer, The Good Parson
[47] Robert Southey, The Morning Mist

185

When I reach one of the hollows in the Downs, I put my machine into safe quarters, and then commence to climb the hill, which is covered in short grass and is exceedingly slippery. Here one of the fritillaries, *Aglaia,* is very common. Its flight is rapid, so that on the steep slope it is no easy matter to capture a specimen, for running after it is quite impossible. I notice that some specimens are much brighter than others and discover that the pale coloured ones are battered. By standing still I can secure as many specimens as I should require, but even the bright coloured examples are not in good enough condition to serve as cabinet specimens and I restore them to liberty. By easy stages I reach the top of the hill and before me lies the magnificent and fruitful 'Weald of Kent'. I shall not attempt to describe the extensive view, it must be seen to be thoroughly appreciated, but visions of a future ramble, extending it may be into two or three days, rise into my mind, for to speak truly, I am here on the outskirts of a vast *terra incognita* extending across the centre of Kent.

I descend the hill and by occasionally riding along the Old Pilgrim Road a short distance and then making excursions therefrom into the hollows, I arrive opposite to the little village of Brooke. The shape of the hill here has obtained for it, I believe, the name of the Devil's Bowl. The lower portion of this hollow is carpeted with one mass of marjoram, wild thyme and other sweet-smelling plants in full blossom, and these are the resort of myriads of insects. Amongst them I notice the second brood of the Dingy Skipper *(Thanaos Tagis).* Higher up the hill is a copse, fit residence for a 'warlock'. Autumn has just begun "with his gold hand to gilt the falling leaf[48]" and the berries of the bramble, wild rose and other shrubs assist to give a variety of colour.

> *"And thou wild bramble, back just bring*
> *In all thy beauteous power*
> *The fresh green days of life's fond spring*
> *And boyhood's blossoming hour*
>
> *Again thou bidist me be a boy*
> *More fair than bird or bee*
> *To head in freedom and in joy*
> *O'er bank and brae with thee"[49]*

The ground is strewed with the spreading thorny branches of the dewberry and a plentiful supply of large ripe fruit testifies to the absence of schoolboys.

At length I am reminded that it is time for me to commence my return journey for the sun begins to sink towards the west. I am directed to the 'Honesty' at Brooke for refreshments and arrive at a comfortable inn with the curious sign of

---

[48] Thomas Chatterton, Picture of Autumn
[49] Ebenezer Elliott, The Bramble

'The Honest Miller', where I once more obtain extra attention on account of having come from Margate.

The 'Honest Miller' at Brooke

My researches for the day are over, but not the pleasures of my ramble, for leaving Wye on my left hand I take a short cut through Olantigh Park and ride over the short grass under some magnificent trees, with fine views of Eastwell and Godmersham Parks on the opposite side of the Stour valley.

Olantigh Towers, circa 1890

Canterbury is reached as the curfew bell again tolls from the great tower and soon afterwards the autumn mist commences to rise and eventually blots out the landscape from view.

"The love of Nature and the scenes she draws
Is Nature's dictate[50]"

"What more felicity can fall to creature
Than to enjoy delight with liberty"[51]

---

[50] William Cowper, The Love of Nature
[51] Edmund Spenser, Muiopotmus or The Fate of the Butterfly

Modern directions for Ramble 9

From Margate's Turner Contemporary Art Gallery:

Travel along the seafront on the B2051 (Marine Drive) towards the clock tower

Turn right onto the A254 (Marine Terrace)

At the roundabout take the 3rd exit, onto the A28 Canterbury Rd, and follow this road to the roundabout at Birchington

Take the first exit onto the A28 (Canterbury Rd)

At the roundabout take the 2nd exit onto the A28 (Canterbury Rd)

Follow the A28 around Canterbury to the Wincheap Roundabout

Take the 1st exit

Continue along the A28, through Thanington

At the roundabout, take the 2nd exit, onto the A28 Ashford Rd

Passing Chartham, Chilham, Godmersham and Bilting, turn left into Bramble Lane and on to Wye

At Wye bear left, go over the railway crossing and follow the one-way system along Churchfield Way

Opposite the church, turn right into Church St

At the 'T' junction turn left, into Bridge St

Take the first turning on the right into Oxenturn Rd

After about 3 miles, turn left into Plumpton Rd, passing West Brabourne and into Bulltown Lane to a 'T' junction

Turn right, then at the next 'T' junction turn right again into Weekes Lane

Continue along Weekes Lane, which turns into Manor Pound Lane, to a 'T' junction

Turn left into Canterbury Rd and continue for about a mile

Turn right at the Five Bells Inn into The Street, going straight across at the crossroads, into Canterbury Rd

Continue up the hill into Brabourne Lane to a 'T' junction

Turn left into Stowting Hill

Turn left into Big Pett which turns into Whatsole St

Turn left at Elmsted Court Farmhouse, into Elchin Hill

Continue across the crossroads into Elvington Park Rd, to Hastingleigh

At the crossroads, turn right into The Street

At the crossroads turn left into New Barn Rd

After about 1 mile turn right into Brabourne Rd

After about 1½ miles turn left into The Street, to Brook

Return to the 'T' junction and turn left into Amage Rd

At the staggered crossroads turn right then immediate left into Upper Olantigh

At the 'T' junction turn right into Olantigh Rd

Continue over the railway crossing to the 'T' junction at Godmersham and turn right onto the A28 Ashford Rd

Continue along the A28 to Canterbury then follow the signposts for Margate

CYCLING IN CONTEXT – extracts from contemporary media sources

The following selection of contemporary articles on cycles and cycling covers a period of 30 years (1868-1898) and includes the time our cyclist wrote his journals detailing his rambles around the Kentish countryside (1886). The extracts indicate Victorian attitudes towards cyclists and their machines and include the views of physicians, government, women, cycling clubs, periodicals, and more. Some extracts connect with the trends in Europe and America.

(1868)
Velocipedes – The French Connection

Velocipedes – Anybody who has visited Paris within the last few months cannot have failed to notice the large number of velocipedes going to and fro, especially in the evening; indeed, the number that may now be seen any evening in the Champs Élysées is so large that a recent police edict compels the riders to affix a lamp to them in consequence of the accidents that have happened from their use. According to some investigations that have been made, it has been ascertained that on a good road, where the gradients are not much greater than on railways, the rider may travel for 80 to 100 kilometres in a day, which is about the same speed as the mail coaches used to attain in France; and that this may be done several days in succession, without over fatigue, by a moderately strong man. Very much, however, depends on the perfection with which the machine is constructed. If it is unskilfully made, the fatigue of working it is so greatly increased that it ceases to be a pleasure and becomes an exceedingly laborious exercise. It is not the case, as has been stated, that the rate of speed is in exact proportion of the force employed. On a hard, level road the traction is so small, owing to the narrowness of the wheels, that it runs along with great rapidity by the momentum given to it, and with the expenditure of very little force on the part of the rider. Of course where the roads are soft, or there is a steep hill to ascend, the labour of propelling it is increased in proportion to the depth and nature of the soil and the steepness of the ascent. The cost of the best velocipedes in France is about £12, but they will probably be manufactured at a much lower price in England if they come into extensive use, as is not unlikely, considering that they afford opportunities for vigorous exercise, in addition to the facility with which long journeys may be made by them. As it may some day be deemed interesting to know the name of the inventor of the velocipede, it may be mentioned that authentic records exist showing that Nicephorus Niepce, one of the earliest of the discoverers of photography, wrote from France to his brother, then living at Hammersmith, an account of his having invented the machine – the letters in which he communicated the fact to his brother being still in existence, and bearing the postmark of the two countries – Once a Week.

(The Times Thursday, Nov 19, 1868; p. 3; Issue 26286; Col. F)

(1869)
The velocipede from a medical stand-point

The vast majority of people are almost wholly responsible for their physical condition. Bodily strength and sound health, like mental accomplishments, are the results of cultivation, and the greater part of mankind can as easily obtain them as they can acquire a knowledge of Mathematics in school or college.

Let any one place, side by side, the closely confined student or clerk and the man who has paid special attention to his physical culture. Compare the pale or sallow face, the flat chest, the narrow, stooping shoulders of the former, with the development of the latter, whose vigorous frame defies disease, whose strength gives a consciousness of power that makes him fearless of danger, and who can exult in that greatest earthly possession, exuberant health. These two classes of men will be the fathers of the next generation. The great disparity between them can be obviated by physical training on the part of the former. If not, then, merely as a means of happiness to ourselves, is it not a duty we owe to succeeding generations, that we cultivate these means of raising man to the summit of his nature, physically as well as mentally?

The condition of civilization (if one avoids its vices) does not weaken bodily vigour provided the locomotive system is kept in thorough activity. The masses should not only have the necessary amount of exercise in the open air, but a perfect exercise of every muscle in the body. A neglect of the powers with which our Creator has endowed us is punished by their withdrawal. Allow the intellect to remain idle and it will become sluggish. All parts of the human organism not sufficiently worked are liable to degenerate; the nerve force which should guide and govern is allowed to sleep; the muscles become inelastic fibre of but little vitality. Tie up an arm for months and it withers away. Let the muscles of our young men and delicate young ladies remain idle, they degenerate and atrophy.

Everything that prolongs human life, ameliorates human suffering, elevates and develops the human frame, is an element of progress: an element that all true men admire and cherish. The velocipede is one of the finest inventions of the nineteenth century. It is a physiologically constructed machine; is an invaluable means of promoting health, and bids fair to emancipate our youth from the common muscular lethargy and debility.

Velocipeding is superior to skating, horseback riding, base-ball, and rowing. While skating is good for the legs, horseback riding for the chest, base-ball and rowing for the legs and arms, the benefit derived from exercise on the velocipede is not local. It gives a natural exercise and general development to every muscle of the body. The arms are the first to feel the effect of the exercise, for the pressure of the feet upon the stirrups must be met by a corresponding pressure of the hands on the tiller, necessary to prevent the front wheel from turning. This pressure of the tiller against the hands puts the rider in an upright position, with elbows well back and hands well extended, straightens the stooping shoulders, facilitates respiration, expands the lungs and develops the chest. No position can be maintained upon the velocipede inconsistent with ease and elegance of motion or incompatible with the laws of health.

Some physicians of prominence have pronounced against the velocipede, and one has issued a *pronunciamento* advising young men to shun it, but the majority of the profession give it their hearty and cordial support. Medical men are among its most eager votaries. One of the best physicians in our country, who makes diseases of the lungs a speciality, rides the bicycle two hours a day, and prescribes it for his patients. He considers it a great preventive of that scourge of our climate, consumption, and a grand aid to the development and improvement of the human body. Many busy men of the profession in New York, Boston and other large cities, either have their own machines or ride daily in the schools and rinks. They regard this preparation of iron (the velocipede) as better than any in their Materia Medica.

(The velocipede: its history, varieties, and practice, J. T. Goddard, 1869)

The velocipede

Cycling – serious doubts about health issues

It is not very difficult to understand the sudden popularity of the new exercise – riding the bicycle or two-wheeled velocipede. Any new exercise not excessively tedious or dangerous, and involving a little expense, is pretty sure of a welcome in Western Europe and America, and this particular exercise had numerous recommendations. It requires some skill and activity, without demanding too much, the comparative degrees of proficiency being as marked as in horsemanship or in rowing. It is graceful, or rather there always seems to be in it a possibility of grace, while there is a certainty of attracting attention and fixing it on the performer, which of itself would popularise any amusement with the French, and, perhaps, the English mind. English skaters are not beyond noticing the effect their attitudes produce, and bicycle riding, like skating, combines the pleasure of personal display with the luxury of swift motion through the air. The pursuit admits, too, of ostentation, as the machine can be adorned with almost any degree of visible luxury; and differences of price and, so to speak, of caste in the vehicle can be made as apparent as in a carriage. It is not wonderful, therefore, that idle men sprang at the new idea – we say new, for though the invention is old, it had been forgotten – with a sense of relief, that the infection spread fast from Paris to America, England and, we believe, Russia; that a new trade suddenly sprang up which employs thousands, that the invention was quarrelled for by a legion of mechanicians, that a score of patent suits were introduced into the Courts – one of them in America will be a *cause célèbre* – that riding-schools multiplied by the dozen, that there are races, matches, tournaments on the bicycle, and that we have before us a popular history of velocipedes extending from the dandy-horse of fifty years ago to the last new perfected Yankee notion.

The bicycle is for the moment a rage, but nevertheless we doubt very greatly if it is more; if unimproved it will keep its ground, or become a permanent addition to our means of locomotion. Nothing of the kind succeeds unless it is useful, and the use of the bicycle is extremely problematical. To begin with, there is a serious doubt as to its healthiness. The Lancet, we see, has given a clear though not a very strong opinion in its favour; but the machine has not been tested long enough to decide whether the old objection to it, that it produced a liability to rupture, is entirely unfounded. The old dandy-horse certainly did, and though the strain in using that contrivance was much greater, the feet touching the ground at every step, still the exertion even with the present one is not of the safest kind. Falls, too, are very frequent, and sometimes severe, and a 'run over' is apt to be a serious business, the driver having no horse to bear most of the shock. It is like that very rare and extremely disagreeable accident, the upset of a hansom on its side, an accident which very seldom leaves the passenger unwounded. Then the exertion, though not severe to a strong man in full health, is a great strain on those to whom any such means of locomotion would be most valuable, the men to whom a long walk is a toil and severe rowing an impossibility. It is not a vehicle for women either and the addition of a second seat, which has been talked about, even if practicable, would greatly increase the labour without at all diminishing the chances of an overset, which, disagreeable even to men, would to women be not only dangerous, but frightful, the side of the face being usually the part of the body most injured. This last objection applies also to the tricycle, which ladies can work, as the seat resembles that of a sulky, and the power is applied through treadles. It will turn over, however, if carelessly managed, or if it runs away down hill, or if turned too sharply out of the way of a horse; and the driver, as the writer can testify from experience, is almost invariably thrown on the hands and the side of the head, which strike the ground with unpleasant or, if the speed is considerable, dangerous force.

Still, in spite of all these drawbacks, the tricycle, admitting as it does of a resting seat, might have a great popularity, if only one difficulty could be overcome. Nothing is more wanted in modern life than a means of getting swiftly about on common roads without incessant expense; of going, say, thirty, or even twenty, miles without very great fatigue. Of all the drawbacks to country life, none have been more severely felt than the rapid increase in the cost of keeping a horse, an increase of at least 100 per cent within the last half-century. Whole classes, like the poorer clergy, dissenting ministers, poor doctors, and many more, who want to move about freely, are chained to a narrow circle, because they cannot afford to keep for six days in the week a vehicle they want for only two. Mr Lowe[52]'s budget will in all tolerably populous places remove much of this inconvenience, as very small innkeepers will be able to keep cheap vehicles for hire – a gig, for example, might be let for 2s 6d a day, if the journey were moderate – but still the power of getting swiftly about without fatigue and without cost would, in many places, and too many classes, be invaluable. This is just what no existing bicycle, or tricycle, or velocipede of any kind fully confers. It will not help the traveller up-hill. The labour of forcing it along any ordinary rough road is calculated to be nearly equal to that of walking, the proportions being one-sixteenth as compared with one-thirteenth; but up an incline it is indefinitely greater: greater, in fact, than if the traveller had to carry the velocipede himself, so great that it is easier to walk and drag or push the vehicle before him. In most English counties, with their swelling undulations, and roads built apparently with a view rather to the enjoyment of scenery than to the saving of labour – in a county like Kent, for example, this objection, unless it can be overcome, is fatal to anything approaching the universal use of the velocipede, and it is extremely doubtful if it can ever be removed. Certainly it cannot be while the only power employed is that residing in the traveller himself. No conceivable ingenuity of adjustment can seriously relieve him up-hill, or enable him to get to the top without carrying his own weight and that of his machine. 'Old velocipedists all affirm that it is better and wiser on long journeys to walk up the hills, for there is a much less expenditure of power in walking up the hills and leading the bicycle, or even pushing a four-wheeler, than in attempting to force it along by means of the treadles'. It is to this point we conceive the attention of mechanics should now be exclusively directed. They cannot lighten or strengthen the velocipede much

---

[52] Robert Lowe, Chancellor of the Exchequer 1868-73

more, or enlarge its wheels without greatly adding to its weight. Is it impossible, without giving up the main idea of the velocipede, that the driver's own strength should be the motor, to store up power to aid him when he has a hill to pass or a bit of very heavy road? Steam is, of course, out of the question; it would be too dangerous and too costly; but is there no possible combination of springs, no application of compressed air, no use of the magnet which would secure an occasional and limited addition of power? We must leave the subject to the Engineer or the Mechanic, but we have a recollection of an invention by a Mr Porter, we believe, of New York, which actually drove a railway engine, the motive power being a magnet incessantly cut off and reapplied, and which was abandoned chiefly because it proved more costly than steam. At all events, the real point is, is there the possibility of obtaining fresh and intermittent power to be used only when required? With it, the tricycle might become a valuable addition to our locomotive resources; without it, it must remain, as at present, a toy used by those who like or require very violent exercise, or who have a skating rink or bitumen pavement on which to display their address.

(The Spectator, Volume 42, 1869, pp. 618-19)

"Them queer horses"

A journey on bicycles from Liverpool to London, by way of Oxford and Henley, has just been accomplished by two of the Liverpool Velocipede Club. On Wednesday evening, Mr A. S. Pearson and Mr J. M. Caw, the honorary secretary of the club, set off from the shores of the Mersey for a 'preliminary canter' to Chester, from which city they started in earnest on Thursday morning. After a ride of 59 miles they arrived at Newbridge, near Wolverhampton, where they stayed the night. On Friday the velocipedians, having traversed the Black Country, went on to Woodstock, a distance of 69 miles, where they slept. On Saturday night the tourists arrived in London, feeling none the worse for their long ride. Their bicycles caused no little astonishment along the way and the remarks passed by the natives were most amusing. At some of the villages the boys clustered round the machines, and when they could, caught hold of them and ran behind until they were tired out. Many inquiries were made as to the name of 'them queer horses' some calling them 'whirligigs', 'menageries' and 'valaparaisos'. Between Wolverhampton and Birmingham attempts were made to upset the riders by throwing stones. The tourists carried their luggage in carpet bags, which can be fastened on by strapping them either in front or on the portmanteau plate behind. This is stated to be the longest bicycle tour yet made in this country, and the riders are of the opinion that, had they been disposed, they could have accomplished the distance in much less time.

(The Times, Wednesday, Mar 31, 1869; p. 9; Issue 26399; Col. E)

One hundred miles on a bicycle

In these days of velocipede wonders the following excursions may be considered the greatest feat yet accomplished. On Thursday morning last Mr G. R. Noble, of Thirlby-house, Woodford-bridge, mounted on one of Charles P. Button's improved bicycles and accompanied by Mr H. E. Kaye, also of Woodford, started from the latter place at half past 3 o'clock for Colchester (distance of about 49 miles), where they arrived about 2 o'clock and, in order to make up the 100 miles, they rode in and around the town for about half an hour. After having sufficiently rested, the velocipedists started on the return journey and reached home about one in the morning, having been absent just 22 hours. Seven hours were occupied in taking meals and rest, so that 15 hours were actually spent in the saddle, giving an average of about seven miles an hour for the whole journey.

(The Times, Wednesday, Jun 30, 1869; p. 9; Issue 26477; Col. F)

A Two-Wheeled Steed

I am not ashamed to admit having always cherished a peculiar admiration, at one time amounting to awe, for anything that would go round. A wheel has never been without its charm for me. I remember, at school, the affection with which I regarded wheels of all sorts, and how all my favourite toys as a child were rotary ones. The knife-grinder, who used periodically to stop in front of our play-ground gates to grind the young gentlemen's knives, has probably died without knowing the inward comfort he administered to my breast, through the opportunities he afforded me of seeing his wheel go round at public expense.

Only the other day, I confided to an old friend that I still possessed a sneaking regard for wheels, and though he rewarded my confidence with a pitiful sneer, I know that this wretched old hypocrite himself keeps a wonderful brass top that will spin for an hour, under a glass case on his study table, and in secret delights to watch it in motion.

A clever marine engineer, who loves wheels too, once told me with great gravity that the human mind has never yet discovered anything so wonderful as the principle of the common wheelbarrow, 'an invention', he said, 'to which that of the steam-engine itself is nothing. The wheelbarrow', he went on, 'is the only example I am acquainted with in which the very weight of a load is fairly utilised as a locomotive power'. There was a copy of Punch on my table. Our conversation had turned to the subject of wheelbarrows from looking at Mr Keene's vignette, in which, some three years ago, Mr Punch was depicted as Blondin, but performing the impossible feat of wheeling himself in a wheelbarrow along a tight-rope in the Crystal Palace transept. My engineer friend then remarked that, putting aside the tight-rope business, he was firmly convinced that Mr Keene had in jest represented what would by-and-by be accepted in serious earnest as the only correct principle on which to construct a self-driven vehicle – namely, employing the weight of the body as a propelling power, and relying on the fact of motion as the means of balance. One thing will at least be conceded by any person who will take the trouble to turn to the sketch, and that is, notwithstanding all recognised notions and experience to the contrary, the picture of a man driving himself in a wheelbarrow looks strangely plausible, probably from the fact, that the mind of the observer communicates motion to the wheel, and is satisfied to receive that as the explanation of the balance.

The two-wheeled velocipede or bicycle is in part a realisation of Mr Keene's picture. It depends upon motion for its balance. The two wheels, one in front of the other, with a saddle between, whether mounted by a rider or not, will not stand upright for a single instant at rest; but, like the boy's hoop, being kept rolling, they maintain a perfect equilibrium.

The bicycle can hardly be called a 'new invention', being to a great extent a modification of that very old toy-vehicle of our fathers, the hobbyhorse, whereon the rider used to sit and row himself along, so to speak, by paddling with his feet on the ground; at the same time, the entire reliance on the principle that motion would be, under any circumstances, sufficient to produce balance, is sufficiently novel almost to justify the use of such a term. The French appear to be entitled to whatever of credit attaches to the original invention of the hobbyhorse (a miserable steed at best, which wore out the toes of a pair of boots at every journey). M. Blanchard, the celebrated aeronaut, and M. Masurier conjointly manufactured the first of these machines in 1779, which was then described as 'a wonder which drove all Paris mad'. The French are probably justified, moreover, in claiming as their own the development of this crude invention into the present velocipede, for, in 1862, a M. Rivière, a French subject, residing in England, deposited in the British Patent Office a minute specification of a machine identical with that now in use. His description was, however, unaccompanied by any drawing or sketch, and he seems to have taken no further steps in the matter than to register a theory which he never carried into practice. Subsequently, the bicycle was re-invented by the French and by the Americans almost simultaneously, and indeed, both nations claim priority in introducing it. It came into public notoriety at the last French International Exhibition, from which time the rage for them has gradually developed itself, until in this present 1869 it may be said, much as it was a century ago, that Paris has again been driven mad on velocipedes.

Extensive foundries are now established in Paris for the sole purpose of supplying the iron-work, while some scores of large manufactories are taxing their utmost resources to meet the daily increasing demand for these vehicles. The prices of good serviceable velocipedes range from two hundred and fifty to four hundred francs (ten to sixteen pounds), at a less price than which a really good machine cannot be obtained either in England or France. The best French pattern is that of Michaux et Cie, which is the one now adopted by most of the English builders with more or less correctness. The height of the driving-wheel most suitable for general use is three feet.

The advantages of the bicycle over the three and four wheeled velocipedes are many and considerable. It is less than half the weight of the old machine, being but a little over forty pounds; and the friction is reduced to something like two thirds. The power, operating directly on the cranks instead of being communicated through long levers, is wholly utilised, whilst the motion of the feet is more analogous to that of walking. When once accustomed to the use of the two-wheeled velocipede, it is not at all fatiguing, whereas the many-wheelers condemn their riders to a term of hard labour. As the result of several months' experience in driving a bicycle, I have no hesitation in estimating it as a clear gain of five to one in comparison with walking; that is to say, the rider may go five miles with the same expenditure of labour as in walking one, and after a journey of fifty miles he will feel no more fatigue than after having walked ten. Notwithstanding appearances to the contrary to the unaccustomed eye, the bicycle is, moreover, a safer machine than any velocipede with three wheels, and far more under control. To turn a corner with a three-wheeler at anything like speed, is a most hazardous experiment, resulting almost certainly in a 'spill' – because the speed lifts the hind-wheel describing the outermost circle, from the ground; whereas the two-wheeler, when on the turn, stands at an inclination like a skater's body, more or less acute according to the quickness of the curve to be described.

With regard to the speed which may be attained, fifteen miles an hour, under the most favourable circumstances, that is, good hard road, not level, but without very steep hills, and no wind blowing, is probably the limit of the velocipede's powers; but a pace of nine or ten miles an hour may be maintained for five or six hours without distress. Long journeys on level road are perhaps the most fatiguing, on account of their monotony, because then the feet, as in walking, are nearly always at work. Still, even in this case, the driver can maintain his speed with one foot, resting the other on the leg-rest; or, if disposed, he may even place both feet on the rests, and run four or five hundred yards without working at all. The slightly increased labour of climbing a hill is nothing to the zest imparted by a knowledge that there is sure to be a hill the other side to go down, and that is the most luxurious travelling that can be imagined. Descending an incline at full speed, balanced on a beautifully tempered steel spring that takes every jolt from the road – wheels spinning over the ground so lightly they scarce seem to touch it – the driver's legs rested comfortably on the cross-bar in front – shooting the hill at a speed of thirty or forty miles an hour – the sensation is only comparable to that of flying, and is worth all the pains it costs in learning to experience it. The velocipedist feels but one pang when he reaches the bottom of a hill, and that is, that it is over; and but one exquisite wish, which is, that the entire country might somehow become metamorphosed into down-hill. But the hill is bountiful even after one has left it, for the impetus derived from a good incline will carry the rider at least the hill's length on level ground before he need remove his feet from the rests and commence working again. The slightest incline on a good road is sufficient to obviate all necessity for working with the feet, so that what little labour there is (and it is of the easiest), is by no means incessant. In a journey of twenty miles on good road, a driver should not work more than twelve – the inclines do the rest. Of course, there are hills so steep that to ascend them is impossible: yet, for myself, living in a hilly county, which I have pretty well explored on my two-wheeled steed, I can reckon up their number on the fingers of one hand. There are also hills where the labour becomes as much as, or more than, walking, but these must be of a gradient something like one in twelve, and such hills are not frequent. When they do occur, the rider may, if he will, dismount. It is a subject of smiling pity to many of the uninitiated to behold a velocipedist dragging his horse after him up a hill – and cruelly realised, too, in the case of three and four wheeled machines; but the bicycle is better than any walking-stick to assist a person up an incline, even when only walking beside it. Resting one elbow on the saddle and leaning the weight of the body on that, while guiding the handle with the other hand, the machine becomes a positive assistance instead of an encumbrance. This sounds like fiction, but it is fact. *Experto crede.*

There are persons who advertise to teach the use of the velocipede in 'a few hours'. Not long ago an enterprising French master advertised to teach the French language (in the intervals of seasickness) during the voyage from Dover to Calais. It should not be concealed that it requires as much time to learn the use of the bicycle as to learn to skate – and there are also occasional falls incidental to learning either. To urge the time necessary to acquire its use as an objection against the two-wheeled steed, would, however, be manifestly unjust. So difficult is it to balance the human body on merely two small legs and a pair of feet, in an upright position (a position such as would be scarcely possible to make an exact model of a man, even without life, retain for a single instant), that it has taken most of us a twelvemonth to learn how to do that. It is sufficient to say that a person may attain the management of a two-wheeled steed in less time than that of a four footed one and when he has done so, for speed, endurance and inexpensiveness, the former will at least bear favourable comparison with the latter. As in skating, a week's steady and persevering practice is needful to acquire a comfortable balance and gain control over the unaccustomed form of support. The 'falls' referred to above as happening in learning the velocipede, are nothing to those incurred in learning to skate. No one should mount a bicycle until he is acquainted with the way to get off, which is really the first lesson. Whichever way the machine is going to fall, the learner has only to put out his foot on that side. His foot being not more than three inches from the ground, the horse, in the act of falling, will deliver him safe on *terra firma,* if he will only let it, whilst, by retaining his grasp of the handles, the rider at once balances himself on alighting and saves the velocipede from falling.

Some difficulty in remounting without help is sure to be experienced by a learner. For a month he must content himself with the assistance of the first post or gate or palings he sees by the wayside; but he will soon discard such assistance and be able to vault on the saddle whilst his horse is in motion. Good hard road is essential for velocipede-driving. In muddy or loose gravely road, the work becomes proportionately laborious. But with good 'going ground', it is difficult to convey how little labour is really required to maintain a high rate of speed – in fact, the great trouble with beginners is to get them to restrain the expenditure of muscular force. Velocipede-driving is, I believe from experience, most healthy and exhilarating, since it exercises all the muscles of the limbs in a manner much more uniform than would at first be credited and certainly without undue strain on any part of the body. To the spectator, the velocipedist appears almost wholly to employ his legs, but in reality the muscles of the arms are in strong tension in the act of grasping the handles so as to counteract the motion of the feet on the pedals, which motion would otherwise tend to sway the wheel from side to side. In fact, after a long journey, the driver will feel more fatigue in his arms than in his legs. Once mastered, the two-wheeled steed is a docile and tractable animal, equally sensitive to bit and bridle and a sturdy friend to the traveller. For him the pike-men throw open their gates without asking for toll. He needs neither corn nor beans nor hay nor straw, neither ostler nor stableman. His stable is a bit of the passage-wall, against which he reposes without taking up any room until his master needs him again – his only food, a pennyworth of neat's-foot oil per month.

There is a Japanese sauce surnamed the 'Maker to Eat'. It will have little charm to the palate of him who drives a bicycle; for, be he the veriest epicure of the epicurean sort, he will, after a three hours' run, possess an appetite to which the most homely bread and cheese appears dainty.

At present the bicycle is regarded, in England, very much in the light of a toy and its practice as a pastime: not so in Paris and New York, where persons of all grades may be seen solemnly and seriously going to their daily business on two wheels. Now that the supposition about the new velocipedes frightening horses has been proved to be groundless, there seems little reason to doubt they will become equally popular in this country; and that after the first rage for the novelty has died away, the two-wheeled steed may drop into its proper place as a serviceable nag that can do a great deal of work in a very little time and, after the first cost, at a very inconsiderable expense.

(Chamber's Journal of Popular Literature, Science and Arts, William Chambers, Robert Chambers, 1869, pp. 280-282)

(1870)
The Bicycle – Just a Toy?

Sir – As various letters on the 'Bicycle' have lately appeared in the English Mechanic, all very much in favour of this new machine, I think a few words from myself – I having been in continual practice for over twelve months – may be of some interest and save much disappointment to those of your readers who are about to learn.

Some time back, at the first introduction of these machines, I, Herman Sloman and others, while advocating the use of them for amusement and exercise, deprecated their utility for practical purposes or economising force. A correspondent at that time calculated theoretically the difference between bicycle riding and walking; he concluded an elaborate calculation proving that the force necessary for walking a distance, say five miles, if put into use on the machine, would only carry three miles, or little over two thirds. These calculations were based on the fact of the bicycle not taking the rider, but vice versa, the rider pushing the machine, of which, by experience, I am painfully aware.

I have travelled most of the Surrey and Kent main roads and find (with the bicycle), taking the roads as they come and using force enough to thoroughly exhaust myself on a twenty mile journey, an average of about four miles an hour to be the outside speed, I can continue the journey – this being less than my walking pace. The machine I ride is a 38in. wheel; my height is 5ft 10in.; weight 11 stone. On a walking tour I manage generally to do about 30 to 40 miles a day, which, up to the present I have not been able to do on the bicycle; although, had I trained twelve months for a walking expedition, I am satisfied 50 miles within the 24 hours would be rather under than over my power of endurance. My experience makes me believe that those of your correspondents who write of travelling 15 miles an hour on the bicycle must either be joking, or totally unacquainted with the subject. I will admit that on a level asphalt road, say a quarter of a mile round and perfectly level, a very high rate of speed may be obtained; and so it is with the locomotive, which on a plain road travels at 10 miles an hour, but on rails, where the friction is reduced to a minimum, 40 miles is done easily. I therefore consider the bicycle a toy and only fit for exercise; although there are some men particularly fitted for these exercises, which perhaps may explain some of the astounding feats of which we read; but I find, on enquiry amongst my friends, that the majority join me in discarding the machine for all practical purposes.

If enthusiasts think it necessary to have a manual machine for utilizing force, I cannot recommend them anything better than a round wire cage similar to that of the squirrel; by imitating the movements of that industrious little animal, they may produce motive power to their hearts' content. A wheel-barrow, also, would do, but has the disadvantage (as some bicyclists say) of not utilizing the weight of the body. I can quite agree with your sensible, but facetious correspondent, 'W.', who on a long journey thinks it better to carry the bicycle; and I am perfectly satisfied, joking aside, that on ordinary hilly and dusty roads it is much easier to walk behind and push the machine with the hands than to mount and force it forward by using both hands and feet.

R. G. Bennett.

Sir – I have read, with some surprise and considerable amusement, a letter from Mr R. G. Bennett, in your issue of the 12th inst., in which he asserts the bicycle to be a mere toy and useless for all practical purposes. This opinion he alleges to be derived from twelve months' experience of the machine, during which time he has not attained an average speed of more than four miles an hour, 'using force sufficient to thoroughly exhaust himself on a twenty-mile journey'. That Mr Bennett's statement is true as regards himself, I am, of course, bound to allow; but that it represents the general experience of bicycle riders, I most emphatically deny. That he has failed in accomplishing in twelve months what ninety-nine persons out of a hundred could do in three weeks, I can quite believe; but I am bound to protest against his holding up his own lamentable failure as a scarecrow to intimidate others from learning the machine.

The bicycle club to which I belong always travels at the average of eight miles an hour for the whole journey. When the road is down hill, we frequently run, for some two miles, at the speed of twelve to fifteen miles per hour; uphill, we work at from four to six miles an hour; on level roads at seven to eight, or even nine miles an hour if the ground is smooth. If I go out with only a single companion, I travel faster than this, as the delays incidental to a large number riding together do not occur.

Mr Bennett calls to his support the testimony of a correspondent, who, he states, 'proved', some time since, by an 'elaborate calculation', that the force necessary for walking a distance of five miles, if put into use on the machine, would only carry three miles, or little over two-thirds. I have no doubt that a person who 'proved' three miles to be a little over two-thirds of five, would be capable of proving anything; and in any matter of theory, I should certainly beat a retreat from so unscrupulous an arithmetician. But I should be most happy to afford Mr Bennett the opportunity of practically testing the 'elaborate calculation' before mentioned, by matching my bicycle against his legs for a day's journey. I may mention for his comfort, that I could travel sixty miles in a day with the greatest ease (I have ridden forty miles after five o'clock in the afternoon); and as I should have to work as hard to get three miles as he has to do five (*vide* the 'elaborate calculation'), it follows, of course, that to prove this theory he would require to walk one hundred miles a day. I hope he can. I may add that I am by no means a first-rate rider (compared with others in the club to which I belong), nor am I either physically or constitutionally strong; and again, I have not had anything like twelve months' practice.

I cannot, of course, account for Mr Bennett's ill success in utilizing the bicycle and the consequent striking difference between his experience and mine, no more than I can account for the fact that I am unable to swim a dozen yards, though I have been learning for years and go into the water a hundred times in a season, while others acquire the art almost instinctively. But this is no reason why I should set down swimming as a useless and unprofitable pursuit, or assert that no one can swim a great distance because I cannot myself get the length of a London bath. It is quite sufficient for me to know that most persons can learn swimming with ease and that my failure is entirely exceptional and of course owing to my own dullness. I would have Mr R. G. Bennett take to himself the same comfort.

W. E. Maverley

Sir – Your correspondent R. G. Bennett is wrong in supposing that I said it would be better on a long journey to carry the bicycle. I never made, nor should I ever think of making, such an absurd statement. I can, however, bring the testimony of a year and a half's bicycle riding to bear out the general tenor of his remarks, which are, nevertheless, in my opinion, a little too condemnatory of the machine. As Mr B.'s letter is sure to evoke answers from lovers of the bicycle, I trust you will allow me to make a few remarks on the subject in order that your readers may hear both sides of the question from those who have had real experience in the matter.

Every one will admit that the best means of locomotion under the greatest diversity of circumstances, such for instance as the crossing of rough country, is to use the legs with which nature has provided us, supposing of course that the motive power is supplied by the traveller himself. Our natural powers of locomotion are intended to be, as they in reality are, perfect in their adaptability to diversified circumstances. It is under particular circumstances that art steps in and for the time being, supersedes nature. Thus a locomotive carries as easily and quickly over an iron road, on which a man could not walk any quicker than on a grass field – the particular circumstances in the present case being of course the smoothness and hardness of the road. If the velocipede question be viewed in this light, the whole matter may be summed up in a few words.

Presuming that we have good machines (and I think they are sufficiently good), are the particular circumstances of the case, or, in other words, is the quality of our roads such as to give bicycle riding the advantage over walking to the majority of people? I maintain that the true answer to this question is not to be looked for from those few athletic individuals who, if the bicycle was twice as hard to work as it is, would still go tearing about to the risk of their necks; neither ought we to accept the testimony of those who naturally speak in favour of the machine, because they happen to live where the roads are as smooth as a board. The real answer to the bicycle question can only be given by the general public and their opinion can only be measured by the use which we see can be made of the machine. It is now about a year since I wrote and predicted the decline of the bicycle fever and I think we need only look about us to see that it is already taking place. For my own part, I now only see one or two bicycles where I used formerly to see a score and my observations extend over a pretty considerable area. The fact is the machine has utterly failed to establish its utility either, as Mr Bennett says, for practical purposes, or for economising force. On the first appearance of the bicycle in England, it was supposed to be everything that one could wish. It was to be ridden at the rate of 8, 10, or 12 miles an hour and was, in fact, to go almost 'by itself'. The experience of a couple of years has I think, dispelled the illusion and the instances in which the bicycle is put to any really practical use, such for instance, as a business man travelling to and from his office, or a postman carrying his bags, are remarkably rare. The machine is almost exclusively used either by those who are young and strong and who find pleasure and benefit in active muscular exertion, or by those who merely use it for the sake of practising 'fancy' riding and for showing off their skill in such feats as standing on the saddle.

If anyone buys a bicycle with the hope of, with ease and comfort, getting any practical use out of it on our roads, just as they happen to come, I am afraid he will be doomed to disappointment and will be like many others, who, buoyed up with the same hopes, have made a like investment of hard-earned money and would only be too glad to get it back again into their pockets. I do not attribute the failure of the bicycle to the machine itself, though there is ample room for improvement on this point, but to the state of our roads. Let the road surveyors lay us down an asphalt path from town to town and I will undertake to say that the use of the bicycle will be as common as that of a horse and trap.

With regard to the rate of speed at which a bicycle can be driven, I quite agree with Mr B. that some of your correspondents speak in a very random way. They talk, for instance, of riding ten miles an hour. Do they mean that they can really keep up that speed for any distance, say for ten or twenty miles; or only that they can for a short distance ride at the rate of ten miles an hour? I fancy the latter is the real state of the case. Very few riders can, I am sure, keep up a higher rate of speed than six or seven miles an hour for any distance. I have frequently travelled eleven measured miles, containing a fair amount of up and down hill, in an hour and a quarter and from my own experience I am perfectly certain that the same rate of speed could only be continued by a practised athlete. If every man in the kingdom learnt to ride a bicycle, I very much doubt whether the average rate of travelling would exceed four or five miles an hour. I am quite aware that Messrs Jones, Brown and Robinson have occasionally gone 100 miles in a day and have, moreover, appeared at their desks the next morning as if nothing had happened – their spirits, no doubt, being kept up by the pleasing thoughts of seeing themselves immortalized in the papers; but performances of this kind may very well be classed with such feats as walking 1,000 miles in 1,000 hours. A sensible man would undertake neither the one nor the other and neither the one nor the other could be performed without the expenditure of a very considerable amount of vital energy, which would require a great deal of rest and food for its proper restoration.

If the machine is good, the road very smooth, the wind not in the face and the rider strong and healthy and fond of muscular exertion, he may, with ease and comfort, get some substantial use out of the bicycle; but just in the same proportion as one or more of these favourable conditions fail, in just the same proportion does bicycle riding become a 'toil of a pleasure'; and it is the improbability – I may almost say the impossibility – of making these favourable conditions universal, that renders impossible the universal adoption of the bicycle.

W.

('English Mechanics and the World of Science', Volume 11, Aug 26 1870, pp. 543-4)

In collision with the law

Bicycles are pretty generally voted nuisances, but it is only recently that the strong arm of the law has stretched forward to arrest their progress. It was, in fact, only one day last week, that a bicycle, which had spent an evening in careering around Vincent square to the terror of the pedestrians, finally tilted a policeman in the stomach and was forthwith 'run in', with its owner on it to the nearest police-station. Mr Selfe very properly fined the bicyclist ten shillings and cautioned him as to his future proceedings, but we fear the one example will be insufficient. Bicycles are seldom abroad till the evening when the lamps are being lit and in the twilight scatter confusion in the quiet West-End neighbourhoods. Now that a policeman has been butted, something has been done towards putting down the nuisance, but the fine of ten shillings will, we fear, be an insufficient warning. Let us hope that we shall not have long to wait before an alderman gets run over, or a police magistrate mutilated about the toes, when a month's imprisonment, without the option of a fine, will settle the question and once and for all put a stop to men and boys damaging their neighbours without let or hindrance to the top of their bent.

(Tomahawk: A Saturday Journal of Satire, Volume 6, Arthur William A' Beckett, 1870, p. 166)

Sir – Although I am not a bicycle rider – simply because I am an old man – will you allow me to say, on behalf of young men, one word in favour of it? Let me ask, for what purpose are saddle-horses usually kept? Is it not, for the most part, for healthy exercise or for amusement? Of course, not exclusively so. The farmer and the soldier mean use in riding their horses, but there are thousands of young men who have no hope of ever being able to keep a horse, to whom the delight of whirling along on their bicycle is, perhaps, even greater than that of those who can keep a horse. I was astonished and delighted a few days ago at seeing a man, apparently between thirty and forty, with the most astonishing command over his bicycle. It must be comparatively easy to guide it when tearing along on a level road, but the rider that I saw was moving very leisurely through the crowd that one usually sees about the station near the bathing-place at Ramsgate; he was really 'walking his horse', and occasionally stopped to look about him, apparently without an effort, keeping the two-wheeled machine balanced. It was a beautiful one to look at, with a little step by which to mount; and, moreover, the rider had evidently 'come into town on business', his purchases being strapped safely on the spring. I know a young apprentice in my own neighbourhood whose master – a wheelwright – made a bicycle and the young fellow goes many an errand thereon to save time and when he gets a holiday, instead of lolling about, or even going on an excursion by rail, mounts his master's bicycle and makes pleasant expeditions about the country, which otherwise he could not do and to places of interest where 'the rail' would not help him. If a little fatigue is incurred, what then if you cannot do everything on a bicycle that you could do in a 'trap', what then? I am astonished that more young men do not get a bicycle. Old as I am, I think I must begin.

Senex

(English Mechanics and the World of Science, Volume 11, 1870)

(1880)
230 miles without dismounting

The six days' bicycling competition, commenced on Monday last at the Agricultural Hall, Islington, produced a much less brilliant finish than might have been expected from the result of the first three days' proceedings. At midnight on Wednesday the leader, C. Terront (champion of France), had ridden 746 miles 6 laps, thus beating the previous best performance for 54 hours, made by G. Waller, by 2 miles 3 laps. Unfortunately for those who are always on the watch for unprecedented records, Terront subsequent to that period had no occasion whatever to ride at top speed, as none of his opponents were able to make up any of their leeway. Thursday, therefore, saw a considerable falling-off in the number of miles accomplished by the foremost division. Notwithstanding, the day proved full of incidents. H. Higham, of Nottingham, who had been taken ill on the first day, re-appeared and expressed his determination of beating Waller's time – 6 hours 27 mins – for 100 miles made in the September of last year. This he succeeded on doing by 1 min 50 secs, and then set himself the task of defeating H. Andrews's continuous ride of 222 miles 4 laps. In this also Higham was successful, covering in 10h. 59m. 30s. 230 miles 2 laps, without having once dismounted from his bicycle. The other feature of Thursday's proceedings was the collapse of J. Terront and the consequent improved position of W. Cann, C. Homey, W. Shakespeare and H. Andrews. At the close of the day the record stood – C. Terront, 955 miles 3½ laps; Edlin, 850 miles; Cann, 760 miles; Homey, 709 miles 3½ laps; Shakespeare, 678 miles 1 lap; J. Terront, 650 miles; Andrews, 570 miles; Higham, 380 miles 3 laps. A large number of persons assembled on Friday, but beyond the occasional spurts on the part of some of the competitors there was little to interest them. J. Terront did not resume work, and in his absence Andrews took sixth place. With this exception, however, the positions remained unchanged, the following showing the number of miles covered at the close of the fifth day:– C. Terront 1,156 miles 2 laps; Edlin, 1,030 miles; Cann, 934 miles;

Homey, 882 miles 5 laps; Shakespeare, 836 miles; Andrews, 670 miles; J. Terront, Higham and Palmer having retired. There was so great an element of certainty about the result that the first day's proceedings were robbed of all interest. Still, a fairly good number were present, especially in the evening. The pace adopted by most of the contestants was very moderate, although inducements were held out to cause them to increase their rate of progression. Shortly after 10 the contest was declared at an end, the final score reading as under:– C. Terront, 1,272 miles; Edlin, 1,154 miles; Cann, 1,076 miles; Homey, 1,038 miles 2 laps; Shakespeare, 966 miles; Andrews, 712 miles 5 laps. During the week a bicycle, the invention of D. Sparrow, was exhibited, for which it is claimed that it can be ridden by ladies in their ordinary attire.

(The Times, Monday, Mar 22, 1880, p. 6, issue 29835; Col. F)

(1882)
The five miles tricycle championship

This event was held under the management of the Bicycle Union at Crystal Palace, on Saturday. The weather was uninviting, and the attendance of spectators consequently small but a fairly large number of competitors entered, and the contest may therefore be regarded as fairly representative for a sport in its infancy. Owing to the width of the machines it was decided to start only 2 in each heat, and three rounds were necessary, yet even then matters were not settled without difficulty, H. W. Gaskell, Ranelagh Harriers, lodging a protest against M. J. Lowndes, Congleton B.C., for riding so wide as not to give him room to pass. He afterwards, however, withdrew the protest when he found that his opponent would be disqualified absolutely, and not merely cautioned. With this single exception everything passed off satisfactorily, and the Bicycle Union must be congratulated on the success of their new venture, which will, no doubt, be the first of a series. Brief details follow:– **Heat 1** – M. J. Lowndes, Congleton B.C., 1; F. G. Dray, Brixton Ramblers B.C., 2 – won very easily in 18 mins 49⅗ secs. **Heat 2** – H. W. Gaskell, Ranelagh Harriers, rode over in 18 mins 31 secs. **Heat 3** – P. T. Lechford, Finchley T.C., 1; Gustav Schultz, Brighton Cycling Club, 2 – won by 300 yards. Time 19 mins 50⅗ secs. **Heat 4** – C. E. Liles, London Athletic Club, 1; C. W. Coe, Brixton Ramblers B.C., 2. **Heat 5** – T. R. Marriott, Nottingham B.C., 1; A. Woodhouse, London T C., 2. After half the distance had been ridden the Nottingham representative drew right away and won anyhow, the Londoner giving up. Time 19 mins 45 secs. **Heat 6** – A. Dixon, London T.C., rode over in 19 mins 34⅘ secs. **Second round: Heat 1** – Lowndes, 1; Gaskell, 2 – won by five yards. Gaskell lodged a protest against Lowndes on the grounds of foul riding, but afterwards withdrew it, feeling sure it was accidental. Time 17 mins 56⅖ secs. **Heat 2** – Liles, 1; Lechford, 2. Liles waited with his man until within a mile of the finish and then dashing to the front, won easily by 120 yards. Time 18 min 33 secs. **Heat 3** – Marriott, 1; Nixon, 2. Won, after an exciting struggle, by 10 yards. Time, 19 min 11⅖ secs. **Third round: Heat 1** – Liles, 1; Lowndes, 2. The latter showed the way up to the last half mile, when Liles increased the pace and as the visitor could not respond the Londoner passed to the front and won easily. Time, 17 min 31⅖ secs. **Heat 2** – Gaskell, 1; Marriott, 2 – won by 6 yards. Time, 18 min 19⅖ secs. **Final heat** – Liles, 1; Gaskell, 2. Each led alternately until three quarters of a mile from home, when Liles went decisively to the front and finally won a good race by 12 yards. Time, 19 min 39⅖ secs. A medal for the rider other than the winner who made the best time was awarded to Mr J. Lowndes, his fastest being 17 min 56⅖ secs.

Civil Service Bicycle Club

In dull and chilly weather a members' race meeting was held by this club at Surbiton on Saturday when the following results were obtained: One Mile Handicap – J. J. Venables, 225 yards start, 1; R. J. Reece, scratch, 2 – won by 80 yds, in 2 min 52 secs. Half Mile Handicap – H. S. Thompson, 50 yards start, 1; S. F. Smith, 65, 2; won easily. Ten Miles Club Championship – R. J. Reece, 1; T. W. Howard, 2; won by 400 yards. Time, 33 min 15 secs.

(The Times, Monday, Oct 16, 1882; p. 7; Issue 30639; Col. B)

(1883)
The Surrey Club

Under the superintendence of this club some of the most successful bicycle meetings are held, and, notwithstanding the rainy morning of Saturday, and the consequent heavy state of the grass course, their spring gathering at Kensington Oval did not fall short of those which have preceded it. Towards the close the public were a little more demonstrative than was desirable, and the enclosure was invaded by many whose duty did not call them there. Results are as follows:–

One Mile Open Handicap – M. H. Hay (Queen's Cycling), 135 yards start first; H. F. Wilson (Surrey), 85 yards, second; N. V. Cassell (Baretta), 150 yards, third; B. H. Daunton (Trafalgar), 135 yards, 0; A. R. Lockwood (Surrey), 125 yards, 0; J. C. P. Tacagni (City of London), 55 yards, 0; F. G. Medcalf (St James), 105 yards, 0; H. C. White (Clapham Park), 140 yards, 0; W. Brown (Brixton Ramblers), 60 yards, 0. Won by 20 yards. Time, 3 min 20⅘ secs.

Two Miles Members' Handicap – A. R. Lockwood, 50 yards start, first; E. Tyler, 20 yards, second; B. Russell, 250 yards, third; G. R. Oxx, 50 yards, 0; S. Russell, 220 yards, 0; W. Agate, Scratch, 0. Won by two yards. Time, 8 min 29⅕ secs.

10 Mile Open Challenge Cup Race – H. W. Gaskell (Ranelagh Harriers), first; F. Prentice (Ipswich Bicycle Club), second; F. Moore, (Warstone), third; W. Wyndham (London), 0; J. C. P. Tacagni (City of London), 0; O. D. Vesey (Surrey), 0; A. Thompson (Sutton), 0; O. Crute (Sutton), 0; H. F. Wilson (Sutton), 0; M. H. Jephson (Oxford University), 0; and C. King (Salisbury), 0. Won by 10 yards. Time, 42 min 9⅘ secs.

(The Times, Monday, Apr 30, 1883; p. 7; Issue 30807; Col. C)

Tricycles – Better Control than a Horse & Carriage

Sir – Your interesting leader in The Times of today marks a new departure in the fascinating pursuit of cycling. For the first time you demonstrate that a wide distinction should be drawn betwixt the tricycle and the bicycle. Hitherto there has existed a curious confusion in the minds of most people on the subject. Only the other day, when I appeared on my Humber tricycle at the Wimbledon Rifle meeting, I was ordered to dismount at the entrance door and so had to push my tricycle ignominiously to Lady Brownlow's tent, for nearly half a mile over a dusty road way between multitudinous cabs, carriages and four in hands. Now, in reality, logically speaking, it would have been much more reasonable to have made the drivers of these carriages get down and lead their horses, for, beyond doubt, a well made tricycle is much more under control than a horse and carriage. So much, however, cannot be said for a bicycle; unless when in actual motion it lacks stability and thus becomes a source of danger where the space is limited, as is the case of a crowded thoroughfare. Yet, notwithstanding this great and very obvious difference, the powers that be place both machines in the same category and under the same restrictions. One glaring instance of this will suffice: Because Richmond Park had been closed to bicyclists, therefore Mr Shaw-Lefevre declines to allow tricyclists to pass through it.

Some horses, I admit, do not at first like the look of a tricycle, but horses can be accustomed to anything in the way of sight-seeing; witness the manner they work at railway stations; therefore, without going so far as to advocate the admission of tricycles to a place like Hyde Park, I do think the time has arrived for removing the disabilities they at present labour under, so as to give them the same privileges as those accorded to carriages drawn by horses.

I am, Sir, your obedient servant,

A. Campbell-Walker

Ashley House Walton on Thames, Sept 8

(The Times, Tuesday, Sep 11, 1883; p. 10; Issue 30922; Col. D)

Sir – I observe that the police have issued a notice cautioning riders of bicycles and tricycles against racing on the highways and threatening to prosecute any persons guilty of such conduct. As the secretary of the National Cyclists' Union, a body which was founded in 1878 for the protection of the interests of all cyclists and which is the governing body in cycling affairs, I would desire to call attention to the fact that the National Cyclists' Union has throughout discountenanced to the full any such violation of the law as that referred to in the police notice and has, in fact, incurred some odium among a certain number of cyclists by its refusal to be a party to any such breach of the law.

The Union feels that the true interests of cyclists will be best served by its being shown to the general public that riders of bicycles and tricycles are law-abiding, and the Union feels very strongly that any attempts to violate the law in the direction indicated would necessarily lead to restrictions of a harassing character being placed upon the riders of such machines. The Union hopes that all riders will to the utmost support the constituted authorities in preventing any such unlawful conduct.

I am, Sir, your obedient servant,

Robert Todd, Hon. Sec.

National Cyclists' Union, 17 Ironmonger Lane, EC Sept 27

To Colonel Henderson, Commissioner of Police, 4, Whitehall Place, Sept 17

Sir – the National Cyclists' Union have had brought before them a police notice, dated the 3rd September, 1883, relating to bicycle and tricycle racing, and I am instructed to state to you the views of the Union on the subject of such races, in order that in any future communication which the Union may have to make to the authorities, the position of the Union with reference to such racing may be clearly defined.

The National Cyclists' Union is a body which was founded in 1878 under the name of the 'Bicycle Union' for looking after the interests of bicyclists and tricyclists in their relations to the public and to each other. The Union has throughout felt that the true interests of cyclists would be best promoted by strict conformance to the law, and the Union has, therefore, strongly deprecated races being held on the public roads. The following is an extract from the prospectus of the Union:

"It should be clearly understood that the Union does not countenance in any way the infraction of rules or bye-laws, and will not attempt to defend those who offend in this way. For instance, the Union contemplates at no distant date taking

some action against those riders known as 'street pests', who, by their inconsiderate and reprehensible conduct, bring cycling into disrepute."

The Union have always felt that while races on the roads in moderation were very useful as showing the capabilities of bicycles and tricycles, yet this advantage would be outweighed by the fact that if such races were indulged in cyclists might expect that restrictions would be placed on the use of their machines, and that law-abiding citizens would hold aloof from persons who make it a practice systematically to disregard the laws laid down for the regulation of the traffic on the highways of the kingdom.

Some time since a small number of persons, who appeared determined to hold races on the roads, and thus, as it were, to defy the authorities, made serious complaints against the Union for its discouragement of such races, and actually founded a small opposition body for the purpose of carrying on such races. I am sorry to see that such conduct has rendered necessary a notice such as that to which I have referred.

The main object of my letter is, however, to show that road racing is not only not countenanced, but that it is very strongly discouraged by the governing body of cyclists, and to express a hope that, in dealing with cyclists, the authorities will draw a very wide distinction between those who recklessly infringe wholesome regulations and those who are anxious by every means in their power to uphold the law, believing that thereby they serve the true interests of cyclists.

I am, Sir, your obedient servant

Robert Todd, Hon. Sec.

National Cyclists' Union, 17, Ironmongers Lane, EC

(The Times, Saturday, Sep 29, 1883; p. 7; Issue 30938; Col. F)

Sir – I observe a correspondent of The Times advocates the imposition of a tax on cycling machines. Now, Sir, I believe such a tax at the present juncture would not merely be an injustice, but so far as the metropolis is concerned a great mistake and for this reason: The number of horses plying in the streets is enormous, so much so that, owing largely to the neglect of the vestries, London is little better than a huge open stable-yard, plus the dust generated by carriage wheels. Consequent on this state of things the air during dry weather is full of dirt atoms and impure emanations. Anything, therefore, which is likely to mitigate or remove this evil, as well as reduce the drain and strain on horse flesh ought to be fostered instead of discouraged.

I have no hesitation in predicting that when London becomes paved throughout with wood, as it certainly will be, the use of tricycles in our thoroughfares will largely increase. On wood pavements a well made tricycle constitutes one of the most agreeable, quickest and cheapest means of locomotion it is possible to conceive; and in the 'wood time' coming thousands will take to them instead of riding in a cab or omnibus.

Besides, there is this broad distinction in favour of a tricycle: it is not drawn by a horse, but propelled by the individual exertion of the rider himself, who is surely sufficiently taxed by the labour so expended.

I am, Sir, your obedient servant,

A. Campbell-Walker

Army and Navy Club

(The Times Tuesday, Oct 02, 1883; p. 4; Issue 30940; Col. C)

To the editor of The Times

Sir – Permit me to point out another, and certainly not worse, reason than that advanced by your correspondent, who dates from the Army and Navy Club, against the imposition of a tax upon cycling machines. In this town may be seen any day workmen and artisans with their bags of tools at their backs, going to and from their employment, mounted on their 'iron horses', but for whose aid in many instances employment must be lost. In one instance a journeyman blacksmith, living, for his own reasons, in Gotherington, earns his living in Charlton Kings, between which two places lie seven good miles of distance. But for the aid of his bicycle, this man would be compelled to encounter the inconvenience of a change of residence, as there is not sufficient call for his services in the neighbourhood to enable him to fulfil his duty as breadwinner to his family. To tax machines which afford these facilities would be a blunder bordering on a crime.

I am, Sir, your obedient servant

A County JP

Cheltenham, Oct 2

(The Times, Wednesday, Oct 10, 1883; p. 12; Issue 30947; Col. B)

Dr Richardson on cycling

Last night the annual meeting of the Tricycle Union was held at Anderton's Hotel, Fleet-street. The newly elected president, Dr B. W. Richardson, F.R.S., who presided, thanked the union for the honour they had conferred upon him and said that in his vacation he pursued bicycling as a great pleasure and as a greater restorative. He regarded this recreation as one of the healthiest of all exercises and was deeply grateful for the perfection to which the machines had been brought. He deemed it best that the bicyclists and tricyclists should each have a separate and independent organisation for the protection of their rights and the promotion of their interests, seeing that there was a large body of ladies and gentlemen who were essentially tricyclists and nothing else. At the same time, he suggested that there might be a confederation of such societies when they respectively reached 500 members for objects which affected them mutually and their common good. He thought that the days of cycling were now so advanced and its usefulness was so universally acknowledged, that the time has arrived when they should not merely meet for the sake of racing and competing with each other, or to inspect and try new machines. Something should be devised that would appeal to the educational and intelligent part of their nature. While still enjoying cycling as a sport, they could add to the happiness and usefulness of their lives by forming natural history, geological and antiquarian sections and pursuing those studies in the course of their travels. This would especially commend cycling to the parent whose young folk were wishful to become cyclists. The formation of the sections he suggested, if not adopted by that Union, would suitably constitute the basis of a confederation of cyclists which, he thought, would ultimately be established. His desire was that cycling should be not only one of the most delightful and healthy recreations, but intellectually one of the most useful as well. The transaction of some formal matters connected with the organisation of the Union followed.

(The Times, Friday, Nov 30, 1883; p. 10; Issue 30991; Col. G)

(1884)
The Stanley Show – Tandems, Rowing Machines and Folding Bikes

What the Islington Cattle Show week is to breeders and farmers, the Stanley Show week is to the thousands of persons of all classes who take an interest in the improvement of the bicycle or the more varied developments of the tricycle, and the exhibition opened under the direction of the Stanley Club on Monday in the Royal Floral-hall, Covent Garden, bids fair to exceed in popularity its six predecessors.

The large collection of machines and their accessories, such as lamps, bells, patent saddles and modifying gear, includes, it is stated, about 200 different standard patterns of bicycles and tricycles and over 400 specimens exhibited by above 80 different makers and agents. There are few absolute novelties which may be expected to maintain a permanent place in the service or equipment of the cyclist but, on the other hand, there is a very general adoption of a principle of construction which was brought prominently into notice at last year's show in the substitution of double for single driving gear on tricycles.

Again, there is little to note of change or, at all events, improvement, unless it be in workmanship and the fine finish of the bearings in bicycles; though from such returns as can be obtained of the numbers of men who use the two-wheeled machines there is little, if any, falling off in the demand for these 'fliers'. But the popularity of the slower and heavier, though safer, tricycle has grown with surprising rapidity and manufacturers are now directing all their ingenuity and skill to diminish weight and to increase the convenience of the three-wheeled machine: while to meet the sociable desires of new accessions to the ranks of cyclists, they have evolved a four-wheeler with a seat for 'a little one' over the fourth wheel.

What figures a census of the cycling world would show no one can guess, for the unattached – the nomads or casuals – are a very large unknown quantity; but such statistics as are to hand point to the apparent ubiquity of the cyclist. The Cyclists' Union has the support of between 200 and 300 clubs with headquarters in the metropolis and these can show on their rolls some 7,000 or 8,000 members, while it is estimated that there are from two to three times as many clubs in the country. The Cyclists' Touring Club, with its 800 consuls to guard the interests of members and its 1,000 hotel headquarters and recommended inns, can display a still longer list and reckons over 11,000 members on its books.

The two most generally observable of recent modifications in the construction of the tricycle are the arrangements for bringing the driving gear to the centre of the machine and the placing of the steering-wheel in a line with one of the driving wheels, so as to produce what is called a double track machine. Other devices have for object the easy conversion of a sociable into a 'sulky', and the reduction of the width of machines, effected either by a telescopic sliding of the axle, and, in the case of one invention, by the folding at right angles of the cog-wheel driving gear, or by the withdrawal of a movable section of the axle, for the convenience of those whose housing accommodation is limited in extent.

To diminish the difficulties which the crowded streets of a city oppose to the passing of a machine wide enough for two persons to ride in abreast, several manufacturers have contrived tricycles in which the occupants can ride tandem; while for the daring, high-mettled youth there is shown a tandem racing bicycle, the long, straight horizontal bar connecting the saddles having within it a swivel joint intended to save one rider if the other should chance to be thrown over, or, at all events, to lessen the severity of a predestinate 'spill'.

Another modern addition to the power of the tourist to overcome the toils and dangers of sudden steeps in travel is provided in various kinds of differential gear. The most curious novelty of the year is a machine intended to give the rider such exercise for his arms, legs and body as he would get in rowing a boat. This contrivance, which has a sliding seat, is called the 'Oarsman' tricycle. Some of the tricycles exhibited show that a robust rider may accomplish very satisfactory results on these machines. On one, for instance, Mr J. H. Adams, in September last, rode 242 miles in the 24 hours; another has been ridden over 4,000 miles; and Mr T. R. Marriott won the 24 hours' road ride of the London Tricycle Club on a machine with wheels of 42 inches diameter, with a run of 219 miles. The Floral-hall is brightly illuminated in the evening by Jablochkoff electric arc lights. The exhibition closes on Saturday.

(The Times, February 6th 1884, p. 4)

(1886)
The Cyclists' Touring Club – 20,000 members

The annual meeting of this club, which is the largest athletic institution in the world, was held on Saturday night at the Cannon-Street Hotel. Major A. Saville, the president, occupied the chair and remarked the fact that the club possessed a membership of 20,000 persons was a proof that it was popular and was in a flourishing state, while it also tended to show that the sport of cycling was now established on a permanent basis. Mr E. Shipton, secretary, read the report, which stated that the growth of cycling, not only in Great Britain, but also in the colonies, made it desirable for the council to consider some scheme of federation. Efforts were also being made by the council to provide a road book for the United Kingdom, together with a map on a large scale. On the motion of Major-General Christopher, seconded by Mr Todd, the report was adopted. The financial statement, which was also agreed to, showed that there was a net credit balance of £2,071 18s 11d of which £902 was devoted to the reserve fund. A proposal to institute life memberships was discussed at length, the great majority of the speakers being in favour of the proposition. Certain necessary changes of rules were made and the proceedings terminated with a vote of thanks to the chairman.

(The Times, Tuesday, May 11, 1886; p. 5; Issue 31756; Col. D)

(1887)
Bicycle v. Horse

Yesterday, at the Agricultural Hall, Islington, a six days' bicycle v. horse contest was begun for a stake of £300. The bicyclists are Richard Howell, the English champion, and W. M. Woodside, the American champion, while the horsemen are Marve Beardsley and Broncho Charley, the well-known riders from the Wild West Exhibition. The race is not altogether novel, Keen having several times recently ridden against horses at the Crystal Palace. On the present occasion the day's racing is limited to eight hours (2.30 to 10.30 pm). Only one competitor of each side is allowed on the track at the same time. They, however, can change and remount as often as they please. In addition to this contest, Ralph Temple and W. S. Maltby, of America, each day give an exhibition of fancy and 'trick' bicycling and unicycling, while there are several races between other prominent professionals. The cyclists and horsemen do not compete on the same track. The former ride in the inside circuit, which measures eight laps to a mile, while the horsemen on the outside track cover one lap less. There was a large attendance when the race started, while in the evening it numbered about 4,000. Apparently keen interest was taken in the various competitions. Punctually, at half past two the six-days' race began, the first pair being Howell and Broncho Charley. After half an hour Woodside and Beardsley took up the contest. At the end of the first hour the horsemen had a lead of three quarters of a mile. During the second the cyclists overtook their opponents and when the third hour was entered upon they were some 200 yards to the good. The race, however, proved very even and when seven hours had elapsed the score was thus:– Cyclists, 121 miles three laps; horsemen, 121 miles. In the last hour the horsemen did not decrease the distance between them and the cyclists and when time was announced they were more than a mile behind. The scores at the end of the day were:– Cyclists, 137 miles seven laps (Woodside 75.5, Howell 62.2); horsemen, 136 miles six laps (Charley, 67.6, Beardsley 69).

The other races resulted thus:– J. Young, Glasgow, beat H. Patrick, Wolverhampton, in a five miles race for £10. W. J. Morgan and John Keen began a ten miles race for £20, but the latter retired from the contest after going seven laps. Ralph Temple, of Chicago, beat Jules Dubois, of Paris, in a five miles race for £10, after an exciting contest.

(The Times, Tuesday, Nov 08, 1887; p. 10; Issue 32224; Col. E)

The six days' contest between the cycling champions – Richard Howell of Leicester and W. M. Woodside of Philadelphia – and the horsemen, Broncho Charley and Marve Beardsley, of the Wild West Show, was continued yesterday at the Agricultural Hall, Islington. There was no decrease in the interest taken in the race, judging from the immense company which assembled in the evening. The scores at the close of Monday were as follows:– Cyclists, 137 miles seven laps; horsemen, 136 miles six laps. Yesterday, precisely at the advertised time (2.30pm), Broncho Charley and Howell resumed the contest. The horsemen at first decreased the lead of their opponents, but by the end of an hour the cyclists had lost very little ground, the scores at this time being:– Cyclists, 154 miles seven laps; horsemen, 154 miles. Steadily, however, the horsemen made up their lost ground and the eleventh hour of the race found the scores thus:– Cyclists, 188 miles five laps; horsemen, 188 miles two laps. At 195 miles the horsemen got on terms with their rivals. They however, quickly fell behind again and when 12 hours had elapsed they were nearly three-quarters of a mile in the rear. They continued to lose ground for a time. Subsequently the pace of the cyclists slackened and at 239 miles the horsemen again drew level. The racing now proved most exciting. When the last hour was entered upon the Wild West men were two laps ahead. They managed to maintain the lead and when time was called they were rather more than 200 yards ahead. The final scores were:– Horsemen, 272 miles (Broncho Charley 136 miles, Beardsley 136 miles); Cyclists, 271 miles seven laps (Woodside 144 miles, Howell 127 miles seven laps). During the day Ralph Temple and W. S. Maltby, of America, gave an excellent exhibition of fancy and trick bicycling and unicycling. Three matches were also decided as follows:– J. Young, (Glasgow) beat W. J. Morgan (New York), in a five miles race for £10; D. Garners (London) beat Robert Patrick (Wolverhampton) in a five miles race for £10; and Jules Dubois (Paris) beat R. Temple (Chicago) in a ten miles race.

(The Times Wednesday, Nov 09, 1887; p. 10; Issue 32225; Col. A)

(1888)
Cyclists 804 miles, Horsemen 795

At Birmingham, on Saturday evening, the contest between cyclists (R. Howell, English champion, Woodside, American champion and Terront, Paris) and horsemen (Beardsley and Charley, late of the Wild West Show), which had lasted all week, was brought to a close. The conditions of the race were the same as those which governed that at the Agricultural-hall some time ago. It proved a very close contest, but the cyclists in the last few hours gained rapidly and eventually won by over eight miles. The scores at the finish were:– Cyclists, 804 miles 4 laps (Howell 270 miles 2 laps, Woodside 267 miles 4 laps, Terront 266 miles 8 laps); horsemen, 795 miles 6 laps (Beardsley 400 miles 3 laps, Charley 395 miles 3 laps)

(The Times, Monday, Jan 02, 1888; p. 12; Issue 32271; Col. B)

Cycles – the New War Machine

The extent and importance of cycling both as a business and as a sport is well illustrated by the Stanley Show now being held at the Royal Aquarium,

Westminster. It is the eleventh of these annual exhibitions of bicycles, tricycles and their accessories and comprises not fewer than 144 stands, some of considerable extent, representing these machines in every variety and numbering in the aggregate several hundreds. An indication of scientific progress made in these popular vehicles by manufacturers is the mechanical skill brought to bear both in their design and construction, some of their details being highly meritorious as engineering devices.

The increasing popularity of cycling as an art, as well as a pastime, is shown by the fact that no fewer than six publications devoted to its interests are represented, one of which is a German and another a French journal. Novelties there are not a few, but the novelty relates more to detail of construction than to any special departure in design; although there are a few new machines, the most striking departure is the road-sculler, exhibited by Mr F. S. Ruston. The special features of this novel and ingenious machine may be described as the complete adaptation to a tricycle of the rowing action in combination with a sliding seat, as employed in propelling a boat. This has been previously attempted, but so far as we are aware, without practical results. The rider sits as in a boat and propels himself along by the aid of a couple of stirrup handles, each attached to an endless wire rope, one on either side of him. This rope passes over pulleys which are connected by gearing with the driving wheels, the machine being steered at the front by the feet. The force exerted in propelling the road-sculler is distributed over the whole of the body, thereby stimulating a uniform muscular development.

An interesting race took place last autumn in the United States between three crack oarsmen, each mounted on one of these rowing tricycles. A prominent feature on the stand of the Coventry Machinists Company is a hansom cab coolie cycle, which has been constructed by the company for the Emperor of Morocco. It consists of a hansom cab which has a moveable hood and is carried on four main driving wheels with a small steering wheel at front. The cab is propelled by four coolies, who sit in pairs behind the cab, and is steered and braked from the inside. War cycles are prominent in the stand of Messrs Singer and Co., who exhibit fine bicycles, tricycles, and multicycles for military purposes. These war cycles form part of a Government order and are specially constructed. The Victoria war cycle is made up in sections and is intended to carry 12 riders. Each section, or pair of wheels, carries two men, 400 rounds of ammunition and two rifles which can be rapidly detached for use. These machines are the outcome of a satisfactory official trial of Messrs Singer's ordinary touring Victoria at Aldershot during last year. The firm also show a military tricycle of lighter build, constructed chiefly for scouting purposes and capable of carrying, besides the rider, a rifle and 200 rounds of ammunition.

The Scout safety bicycle is another machine designed for war purposes by its exhibitors, Messrs Wilkins and Co. Although comparatively light in weight, it is strongly built and has been satisfactorily tested by being put through some very heavy work, including the ascent and descent of steep declivities and travelling on rough roads. On the stand of Messrs Hillman, Herbert and Cooper is the Premier safety tandem bicycle which is stated to be the first really practical machine of this kind that has been turned out. It can be ridden by one person either in the front or back seat. Two well known cyclists recently tried this machine and with it covered 13¾ miles in 41 minutes. For invalids or others who may desire a pleasure drive, a useful Coventry chair is exhibited by Messrs Stanley and Sutton. It is on the lines of the Bath chair and is driven by a man who rides behind the occupant of the chair. Carrier tricycles are largely represented on many stands and there appears to be a general development in these machines, of which there are many varieties, indicating a wide sphere of usefulness. It is not possible to note the detailed improvements which have been recently introduced by the various makers in their machines, but among other stands where these are to be met with we may refer to the Rudge Cycle Company; Messrs Marriott and Cooper; the Sparkbrook Manufacturing Company; Messrs Bayliss, Thomas and Co.; and the Centaur Cycle Company. Improved spring saddles will be found on the stand of Messrs Lamplugh and Brown and some good cycle lamps on that of Mr J. E. Salisbury. These, with other accessories, complete an interesting and excellent show.

(The Times, Wednesday, Feb 01, 1888; p. 7; Issue 32297; Col. C)

(1889)
Land's End to John O'Groats in Five Days

The Right Hon. The Speaker of the House of Commons attended the Midland Counties meet of cyclists at Leamington yesterday and presided at the luncheon held in the Jephson Gardens. The meet was attended by cyclists from all parts of the country, the Manningham Club, Bradford taking a silver bugle for the club most largely represented at the meet. Mr John Fell, president of the Leamington Club, proposed 'The health of the Speaker', which was heartily honoured. The Speaker, in acknowledgement, said there were some striking facts in connection with the cycling movement. In the first place it had developed to an extraordinary extent the organizing power of the English people. There were about 500,000 people in the United Kingdom who used cycling in some shape or the other. The progress made as a result of that organization struck him as something of which they might all be proud. He did not wish to dwell upon feats that had been accomplished by eminent cyclists, but he was reading only the previous day of one feat that struck him as so extraordinary that he suspected a misprint had occurred in the record. It was stated that a gentleman started from the Land's-end and went to John O'Groat's house, a distance of 861½ miles, in five days, one hour and 45 minutes. Now this was a feat which he did not wish to recommend. They were not all of them physically formed so as to be able to perform a feat of that kind, nor did he recommend fool-hardy feats.

He had been furnished with some records of the best pace in an hour on the road and on the cinder-path. They were always trying to beat the record, from the Atlantic liner down to a runner in a 50 yards race and he did not know when they would stop beating the record, because it appeared to him that every ten years that passed by brought its own record. The machines were getting more perfect, their muscles were getting more inured to the work and the person who sat on the bicycle more part and parcel of it, so that the two became more like one animal. He believed, if he might venture to say a word in support of the Cyclists' Union and of cycling, that they were doing what they could, some more and some less, to promote a healthy and invigorating sport, a sport which had opened up new vistas to this generation, which had enabled them to bear the strain of ordinary daily life and which, he trusted, might conduce not only to the bodily welfare, but to the mental strength of every patron of cycling.

(The Times, Tuesday, Jun 11, 1889; p. 4; Issue 32722; Col. C)

(1890)
Pneumatic Tyres – Will They Catch On?

Stretching away nearly from end to end of the Crystal Palace, expanding into side spaces and filling the concert room and three of the courts, is the finest collection of bicycles, tricycles, and accessories ever seen. This collection constitutes the 13th annual exhibition of the Stanley Cycle Club, the first having been held at the Athenaeum, in the Camden-road, when 60 machines were exhibited. Thirteen years have seen the show gradually expand to one of over 1,500 cycles of various patterns and types besides numerous exhibits of accessories. This is the second year the exhibition has been held in the Crystal Palace, the number of machines last year having been 1,200 and the number of exhibitors 185 as against 230 this year. On glancing at this show the observer cannot fail to be impressed with the remarkable amount of mechanical science and skill which has been brought to bear upon the development of this means of healthy exercise, recreation and sport, and the vast industry the manufacture of these machines has rapidly become. It gives brain work to hundreds and handwork to thousands, and absorbs a large amount of raw material in the shape of iron, steel and coal.

The exhibition does not present many novelties, but it does show an advance in the careful development of the minor details of construction, particularly those which relate to the safety and lightness of the machines and the comfort of their riders. Safety and lightness are largely met by the introduction of steel in the light tubular form wherever practicable, and in the scientific design of the framing, the diamond shape being a favourite form with a large number of makers. In consulting the comfort of riders, springs are introduced in one place or other; by some makers at the axles of either the front or rear wheels and by others at both, while one maker introduces springs into the spokes of the wheel itself. Another novelty is the use of a rubber tyre of very large sectional area, examples of which are to be found on several stands. In one case the tyre is a thick rubber tube 2in. in diameter, while in others the walls of the tube are thinner and the tube is inflated with air. Bicycles and tricycles fitted with this latter tyre are known as pneumatic machines. At one stand the invention was amusingly introduced to our notice by the youthful attendant as the 'dramatic' tricycle. Each of the expedients – inflated and non-inflated – possesses its own degree of merit, but it remains for time and cyclists to determine which is the more meritorious.

Turning from general principles to the machines themselves we will proceed to indicate some of the most noteworthy features of the show, although the task is rendered somewhat invidious by the fact that, with very few exceptions, a high degree of excellence pervades the entire exhibition. Messrs W. Andrews and Co. show a bicycle readily convertible into tricycle for either ladies or gentlemen and a good self-steering safety machine. Messrs Marriott and Cooper have introduced a spring frame into their machines. The same may be said of the Fleetwing Cycle Company's anti-vibration cycles. Juvenile machines are well represented on several stands and notably on that of John Harper and Company (Limited), while Messrs Bayliss, Thomas and Co. have a well-designed ladies' light safety bicycle, one form of which is convertible. The Whippet cycles of Messrs Linley and Biggs are designed to prevent vibration, freedom from which is the main claim reasonably advanced for them. The Pilot Cycle Company introduce a triangulated wheel in which the spokes are twisted one around the other at the outer ring of crossings, a practically rigid wheel, in equal tension at all times, being the result. Messrs Osmond and Co. show a useful heel-clip for pedals which dispenses with the toe-clip. Messrs G. and P. Hookham show their new spring wired tyre, in which a wire is embedded in the elastic tyre which enables a damaged spoke to be repaired by removing a portion only of the tyre from the rim of the wheel. The new features in the machines of the Quadrant Tricycle Company are a spring front wheel, a new saddle spring and a useful spring carrier for photographic cameras.

The most popularly attractive display in the show is that of the Coventry Machinists' Company, in the centre of whose extensive stand is a hansom cab coolie cycle which the company have built to the order of His Majesty the Sultan of Morocco. It measures 16 ft long by 6 ft wide and 7 ft high to the top of the cab. The whole of the framework is nickel-plated, and the body of the cab is finished in light green with gold panels and gold front. The inside of the cab is elegantly upholstered in green and gold. The machine is driven by four coolies sitting in the rear of the cab, but His Majesty has perfect control of the steering and brake power. Inside the vehicle is a case containing a variety of knick-knacks, besides which there are receptacles for sword, field glasses and other articles. Undoubtedly this machine is the most elaborate and costly cycle ever manufactured, the price being 300 guineas. The Coventry Company also exhibit several novelties among their less regal machines. The Crypto Cycle Company have reduced the weight of their machines and now fit three brakes to the tandem instead of two. Messrs J. K. Starley and Co. introduced a new sociable tricycle, in which either a lady and a gentleman or two ladies can sit side by side. Messrs Starley Brothers show the thick-walled hollow tyre to which we have alluded and which they designate the 'anti-pneumatic'. The Humber Company have a novelty in their tandem attachment which can be fitted to any of their tricycles.

An interesting exhibit is to be seen on the stand of Messrs Hillman, Herbert and Cooper in the shape of some military cycles. Their 'Premier' military safety bicycle is in use by the Royal Marine Cycle Corps. It is fitted with clips for holding the rifle and arrangements for carrying the cartridges and valise. The 'Premier' roadster tricycle has been adapted for the use of officers and has a clip for the sword and for a rifle besides fittings for field glass, sketch board, chart, &c. The tricycle is here used, as it enables the officer to stop and take observations and make notes without dismounting. The Civil and Military Cycle Supply also show a variety of war bicycles and tricycles. One of the latest firms to extend and develop their works is that of Buckingham and Adams (Limited), who have recently made large additions to their factory. Their leading exhibit is a very good 'safety' roadster, which has been improved down to date in all respects, including a double-diamond frame. 'Buck-jumper', in connection with cycles, appears rather an incongruous term, or at least to suggest the idea of a bone-shaker of the earlier days of cycling. In reality it is but the distinguishing name of a series of cycles exhibited by Messrs Samuels and Co. who have come over from Amsterdam to show a large variety of very light machines, one weighing as little as 10lb. The Amsterdam firm go in for lady buck-jumpers, their framing, generally, being of the semi-diamond type. The Pneumatic Tyre Agency (Limited) is the chief exhibitor of the pneumatic tyre already alluded to. It is claimed that this tyre deadens all vibration and consequently gives increased speed with less power. The three courts to which we have alluded as being occupied by exhibitors are the Roman, Greek and the Egyptian. The Roman court is occupied by 12 exhibitors, while the Greek court is filled by the Singer Company, who have introduced an improved chain adjustment in all their safety machines. They have also overcome the difficulty of leaning a safety bicycle against a wall, by an ingenious steering lock which defies the most persistent efforts of the machine to lie down. The Egyptian court is allotted to the Rudge Cycle Company, who are introducing a new spring frame and a spring handle. Last, but not least, comes the ingenious safety water-cycle of Mr J. M. Hale, which is a distinct advance in this class of machines. It is either for single or tandem driving and is fitted with the inventor's safety side-floats and his alternately reversed, oblique-bladed propellers.

(The Times, Monday, Jan 27, 1890; p. 10; Issue 32919; Col. C)

223

(1894)
Bicycle v. Skates

Another of these interesting races was brought off at the Hall-by-the-Sea[53] last (Thursday) night and those who were present at this well managed rink witnessed one of the finest and most pluckily fought out struggles that have as yet taken place here. The contestants were A. Page (Margate), skater and G. S. Cousins (Westgate), bicyclist and the race was over the five mile course for a massive gold medal, given by Mr Gus Foster, the enterprising manager of the establishment. The start was made at 8.52, the men being placed at opposite sides of the hall, half a lap (ten to the mile) intervening, Cousins having the rear position. The pace was very fast, the bicyclist gradually, from the first, lessening the distance between them, until just before the completion of the second mile Cousins passed his opponent, being then half a lap to the good. Page struggled manfully and made a good fight for it, but Cousins continued to add to his lead until at the fourth mile he had further increased his advantage by another lap, Page coming on behind in a most determined and undaunted manner. Amidst the greatest excitement the last mile was finished in the gamest fashion, but Cousins held it all his own way and came home the winner.

(Keble's Margate and Ramsgate Gazette, January 1894)

(1898)
"A lady on a bicycle is utterly out of place"

The horse, it has often been observed, is a noble and useful animal, but dealings with him have a demoralizing effect. A bishop, it has been cynically remarked, would get the better, if he could, of his own archdeacon in a horse-dealing transaction; and the evils of the race-course are too trite a subject for mention.

It almost seems as if this ill-repute of the horse is being transferred to that equally useful and far more universal means of locomotion, the bicycle. Its manufacture has of late given occasion to questionable operations of unscrupulous 'promoters', and abnormal profits, leading to over-capitalization, have resulted in the victimization of unfortunate shareholders for the benefit of the fortunate few who share the Tichborne claimant's philosophy, that "some people has brains, and some has money; and them as has money was made for them as has brains."

Its use, too, we are now and again assured, leads to selfishness and disregard of the ordinary courtesies of life. The East-end or suburban 'scorcher' dashing along quiet roads and through peaceful villages with loud shouts and sulphurous language and reckless of life and limb, is not a pleasant development of the

---

[53] Later to become Dreamland

cycling craze; nor are the bicycle thefts that are so easy and so common in crowded thoroughfares; nor, for the matter of that, are the costumes in which some lady cyclists in England are beginning to imitate those of France or Italy. Most real cyclists too and probably every omnibus, cab, van and carriage driver in London, would consider that a lady on a bicycle is utterly out of place in Regent-street or Cheapside, or any other great artery of traffic. The office-boys and clerks who twist in and out among the stream of vehicles, now clinging to an omnibus for support and now darting almost under the nose of a horse, can take care of themselves and a special Providence seems to watch over their wildest escapades; but no one likes to see a woman running unnecessary risk, as it has more than once proved to be, to life or limb.

There is, indeed, much to be said for prohibiting bicycles altogether in the City and in certain streets between, say, 10am and 6pm. But whether any authority, Imperial or local, will have the courage to interfere with so universally popular a pastime and means of locomotion is perhaps doubtful. If the smoker must be conciliated by reducing, unasked, the duty on tobacco, and the anti-vaccinationist by the practical abolition of compulsory vaccination, the cyclist may be able to resist registration, or taxation, or any restriction whatever.

Apart, however, from its incidental drawbacks, there is no question that the bicycle is a social boon – one might almost say in some respects a social revolution. To hundreds of thousands of young men employed in City offices it gives opportunities for enjoying fresh air and wholesome exercise amid a variety of scenery which he never had before, and that at a nominal expense when he once possesses a 'machine'. The London clerk on his Saturday afternoon and Sunday can now range far afield – among Essex cornfields or Kentish hop gardens, or the lanes of Hertfordshire and Surrey; or by availing himself of the assistance of the railway, he may ride like some Homeric hero, 'by the shore of the far re-echoing ocean'. There is, in fact, hardly any limit but that of time to the possibilities of wandering upon the wheels that are open to young men who can travel with all they need upon their backs, or strapped to their machines. And there is no question that their leisure hours are better thus employed than in attending demonstrations in Hyde Park or low class places of amusement. The bicycle may, perhaps, tempt them away from church, but there is no reason in the nature of things, why it should do so. Some clergy on the roads most frequented by Sunday cyclists have arranged services for their convenience with marked success; and the time will probably come when most churches in the country and many in towns will reckon a stand for bicycles as a necessary 'ornament of the church'. In country districts, the bicycle has much facilitated social intercourse, especially among those who have not at command a large stable establishment; and it has made easier the economy in means of transport that agricultural depression has forced upon many country houses. It may even check the tendency to leave the country and gather into towns, which is so marked and, as many think, so regrettable a feature of modern life; and in one very important sphere, that of labour, it is already beginning to do so. The distance from his work is one of the heaviest burdens that the country labourer has to bear. But already there may be seen on country roads labourers of various kinds going to and from their work on wheels; and artisans and others in country towns are beginning to find out that the possession of a bicycle enables them to find cheaper and healthier homes for their families in neighbouring villages than is possible in the town itself. The bicycle cannot, of course, check, but it may conceivably mitigate the decline of the rural population. It has also, as some think, a military future; and the experiment of cycle corps has already met with approval in peace manoeuvres. It has yet to stand the test of actual warfare, under certain conditions of which it would probably be useless. But, given a region of easy gradients and fairly good roads, the bicycle may well do valuable service in outpost and reconnaissance duty, and in transporting small bodies of men rapidly and noiselessly from place to place. And from this point of view, it might increase the effectiveness of the rural policeman, as it already does that of the rural postman.

It is, however, for purposes of summer travel that the thoughts of many of our countrymen and countrywomen are now turning to their bicycles. Along the hot and dusty highways of France, through German forests and over Swiss mountain passes, or, nearer home, alongside the dykes and canals of Holland, that land of absolute yet picturesque flatness, the brethren and sisters of the wheel are even now speeding, happy in the freedom of healthy out-of-door life, and careless of everything but the weather. Nor do foreign countries, as a rule, place difficulties in their way. There is much international fraternity among cyclists and a kind of universal 'Zollverein' of cycling tourist clubs smoothes the way for the members in all lands; and in France, at any rate, the railways have the credit of providing much better and more cheaply than our own for the transport of bicycles. The absurd commercial tariffs of Italy require a heavy deposit at the frontier upon any bicycle of foreign make, to be returned on leaving the country; and perhaps the authorities who, as just announced, feel that public safety is imperilled by a camera or 'kodak' within ten kilomètres of their fortifications will feel equally perturbed at the sight of a bicycle. Who knows but that this knickerbockered young man, or that young lady in a 'divided skirt', may be an emissary of some foreign power, exploring the approaches with a view to the overthrow of the reigning dynasty? But with these slight inconveniences, easily to be avoided, cycling on the continent is probably as free as at home; though it appears that the authorities of Switzerland, of all countries in Europe, have lately been imposing some irksome restrictions – a strange proceeding for a country that prides itself, not unjustly, upon its freedom and its independence of continental militarism, and depends largely for its subsistence upon the strangers who use it as their playground. But neither Swiss authorities nor Italian military officials can do much to discourage a pastime so universal, so well within reach of all, and, we may add, so beneficial both from a sanitary and a social point of view as the use of the now ubiquitous bicycle.

(The Times, 15 August 1898, p. 7, Issue 35595, col. D)

ON THE ROAD TO EMANCIPATION: a female perspective of cycling

Hold on!

(1869)
Velocipede Schools – Ladies Only

The nightly scenes at Burnham's and Witty's schools in Brooklyn constitute quite an interesting entertainment. The expert riders of Brooklyn are multiplying rapidly and at both the above velocipede arenas the displays of skill and daring are numerous. The funny side of the picture is also exhibited nightly in the form of collisions, falls, narrow escapes and the wobbling movements of the tyros in the art. The attendance of spectators each night is such as to crowd both halls, the gallery at Burnham's being specially devoted to the use of ladies and those of the other sex accompanying them, while at Witty's hall the ladies have the front seats. Mr Burnham has introduced velocipede riding as a feature of the exercises of his lady classes and Mrs Burnham already rides with a degree of modest ease and skill surprising to those who imagine that ladies cannot ride a two-wheeled velocipede without objectionable *exposés*. The exercise is especially adapted for ladies and it is simply as an exercise that Mr Burnham has introduced it. None but the ladies are admitted to the hall during the ladies' class exercise and those who have seen Mrs Burnham ride are in a fever to learn the art themselves. The ordinary dress used by ladies on these callisthenic exercises is just suited for use in riding the bicycles, not half as much exposé of the nether limbs being made as in the ordinary walking attire. Never before in the history of manufactures in this country has there arisen such a demand for an article as now exists in relation to velocipedes. They are manufactured now at the rate of 1,000 a week and that is about the tenth part of the number of orders received for them. One contract was made this week for the manufacture of 5,000 boys' bicycles.

(The Times, Wednesday, Mar 10, 1869; p. 5; Issue 26381; Col. F

Velocipedes for Ladies

Early bike for ladies

We present a bicycle for ladies, lately invented and patented by Messrs Pickering & Davis of New York City. It will be seen that the reach or frame, instead of forming a nearly straight line from the front swivel to the hind axle, follows the curve of the front wheel until it reaches a line nearly as low as the hind axle, when it runs horizontally to that point of the hind wheel. The two wheels being separated three or four inches, allow of an upright rod being secured to the reach; around this is a spiral spring, on which a comfortable, cane-seated, willow-backed chair is placed. This machine, with a moderate sized wheel (of thirty to thirty-three inches) will allow being driven with a great deal of comfort and all the advantages of the two-wheel veloce. In mounting, a lady has to step over the reach, at a point only twelve inches from the floor, the height of an ordinary step in a flight of stairs.

A machine for ladies has also been invented by S. T. Derry of Boston and patented by Messrs Sargent and Derry, which in construction and appearance is very similar to the one just described. Its saddle is of velvet on springs, giving a perfectly elastic seat; it is furnished with mud fenders in front and behind and is complete in every respect.

Both these machines have been examined by experts and pronounced satisfactory. It will be readily seen that they obviate many of the difficulties, embarrassments and objectionable features of the bicycle. They will, doubtless, become popular. While young men have been dashing about on velocipedes, many young women have looked on with envy and emulation. They have not been satisfied with the tricycle designed for their especial use; and have felt it hard that they should be denied the exercise, amusement, risk, dash and delightful independence, which the bicycle so abundantly affords.

It is possible that our young ladies will rush into velocipeding as they have into skating and other athletic amusements. It would be a substitute, in many cases, for the expensive luxury of horseback exercise and has the advantages over it of convenience and pleasure as well as cost. Velocipeding will be particularly nice for suburban ladies, who have smooth roads around them, over which they may bowl to their hearts' content and drive themselves from house to house on morning calls. It will not be necessary to keep an ostler, nor to have an attendant to assist in mounting and to accompany the rider. When ready for her ride, a lady may take her horse from the front hall, clean and fresh, mount and be off. It would be a bright and beautiful day for our land, should a laudable and reasonable ambition once fairly get possession of our young women, to cultivate and develop their physical natures and to become strong, healthy, robust and enduring.

A short time since, 'The Revolution' published an able article recommending the use of the bicycle to ladies. It has been used by them for some time in a quiet way and to a much greater extent than is generally supposed. There are classes for ladies in almost every large city and many are waiting for fine weather to enjoy the art in the open air, instead of a closely confined room and to "Witch the world with noble horsemanship[54]".

The idea has been conceived from seeing experts ride side-saddle fashion and drive the machine with one foot, that ladies might begin by learning the art in that way. This would be well-nigh impossible, though it is easy enough after one is proficient. But with a proper teacher of their own sex and with suitable dresses for preliminary practice, ladies can soon obtain such a command over the vehicle that they can ride side-saddle wise with perfect ease.

A lady must begin with great moderation and train her muscles to the work of propulsion, or they will cry out vehemently at first. Above all, she must avoid getting cold, rheumatism and neuralgia, after being heated by the exercise. The best school for ladies is established in Boston and is conducted in a properly private and exclusive manner. It is supplied with a number of lady teachers and assistants, all under the direction of the best 'velocipedagogue' in the city. It is in a large hall in a good locality and is provided with the best French machines, dressing-rooms and other conveniences. Many good old Boston names are to be found upon the list of pupils. The lessons are twenty-five dollars for a course of instruction, with a guarantee of proficiency.

There is also a school especially designed for ladies, at the corner of Fifth Avenue and Fourteenth Street, New York, at what is known as the Somerville Art Gallery. This has two halls of an area of 3,000 square feet. One of the halls is set apart for beginners and the other for those more advanced. Ladies, in riding the bicycle, commonly use the modest and appropriate costume worn by them in callisthenic exercises and in the gymnasium. Another very suitable dress for the *velocipedestrienne* has been thus described:

"Let the outer dress skirt be made so as to button its entire length in front; the back part should be made to button from the bottom, to a point about three eighths of a yard up the skirt. This arrangement does not detract at all from the appearance of an ordinary walking costume. When the wearer wishes to prepare for a drive, she simply loosens two or three of the lower buttons at the front and back and bringing together the two ends of each side, separately, buttons them in this way around each ankle. This gives a full skirt around each ankle and, when mounted, the dress falls gracefully at each side of the front wheel."

Miss Carrie Augusta Moore, well known in amusement circles as 'The Skatorial Queen', has been riding the bicycle in public in Washington, Boston and the Western cities, with much success. Her riding is described as finished and graceful and her costume as neat and modest.

(The Velocipede: its history, varieties, and practice, J. T. Goddard, 1869)

---

[54] Shakespeare, Henry IV, Part 1

Out for a spin

(1896)
On a bicycle in the streets of London,
by Susan, Countess of Malmesbury

A new sport has lately been devised by the drivers of hansom cabs. It consists of chasing the lady who rides her bicycle in the streets of the metropolis. If not so athletic a pastime as polo, the pursuit on wheels of alien wheels surmounted by a petticoat which half conceals, yet half reveals the motive power within, appears to afford these ingenious persons exactly that exhilarating and entrancing sensation without which no Englishman finds life worth living, and which apparently is to the heart of the cabby what salmon-fishing, golf, shooting, the rocketing pheasant, hunting the fox, or, in fine, what war, that highest expression of sport, can be to those who are usually called 'the leisured classes'.

I am given to understand that so far the scoring is altogether on the side of the pursuer. He has bagged, we are told, many ladies whose mutilated or decapitated forms have been hurried into silent and secret graves at the instance of the great Bicycle Boom. Their relatives, we hear, have laid them to rest quietly in back gardens until such time as they can realise what shares they possess in cycling companies. But whether this be true or not – and, after all, the evening papers must live! – if the harmless necessary hansom cabman has gained a new pleasure, he has had to pay for it like a prince; for his former attached and confiding fares, instead of reposing in the comfortable recesses of his vehicles, are now – stout and thin, short and tall, old and young – all alike vigorously ankle-pedalling just on ahead of his empty and sorrowing cab, and right under the fore-feet of his horse. Small wonder, indeed, if he be jealous and sore; and, moreover, it must be admitted that this is one of the irritating habits which the cyclist, male and female, shares with certain of the other lower animals – to wit, with the dog, as everyone knows who has had the blessing of the latter's society in the streets. The way in which he will cross a crowded thoroughfare, mildly beaming round, enjoying the morning air, deaf to remonstrance, within a hair's breadth of a sudden and awful end, is enough to turn the best Auricomous Fluid[55], even, to snow. But I wander from my tale, which is not that of a dog, but of a bicycle.

Having now been the quarry of the hansom cabman for nearly a year and having given him several exciting runs, I cannot help feeling that cycling in the streets would be nicer, to use a mild expression, if he did not try to kill me; although the pleasure which danger always affords to a certain class of minds would be considerably lessened. I should like to say here, as seriously as I am able, that surely it is not right to insult a woman who conforms to the law, to the rule of the road, molests no-one and dresses in accordance with the custom which decrees that she shall at once be distinguishable from those who fondly, yet not with an uneasy lurking suspicion of their true position, claim to be her masters. The English public requires a great deal of educating and as in the days of one's youth certain dates had repeatedly to be dinned into our reluctant ears, so this many-headed grown-up child needs to have certain facts placed before him over and over again, until at last his eyes are opened and behold! He sees.

Prejudice against this kind of locomotion for women has raged acutely, but is now fairly on the wane and it is only in very out-of-the-way streets that one now meets with any expressions of disapproval stronger than 'Trilby!' even from those frivolous and irresponsible persons who have been keeping the feast of St Lubbock[56], not wisely, but too well, or doing that which in France is called *Fêter le Lundi*.

Riding on a track began to bore me as soon as I had learnt to balance, but I remained steadily practising in the modified seclusion of the Queen's Club, where I was taught, until I could turn easily, cut figures of eight, get on and off quickly on either side and stop without charging into unwelcome obstacles. This done, burning to try my fate in traffic and yet as nervous as a hare that feels the greyhound's breath, I launched my little cockleshell early one Sunday morning in July into the stormy oceans of Sloane Street, Knightsbridge and Park Lane, on my way to visit a sick friend who lived about four miles off, beyond Regent's Park. The streets were really very clear, but I shall never forget my terror. I arrived in about two hours, steaming and exhausted, much more in need of assistance than the invalid I went to console. Coming home it was just as bad; I reached my

---

[55] Hydrogen peroxide solution
[56] Bank Holidays; these were introduced in 1871 by parliamentarian Sir John Lubbock, who became popularly known as St Lubbock as a result

house about three o'clock and went straight to bed, where I had my luncheon, in a state of demoralisation bordering on collapse. I only recount this adventure in order to encourage others who may have had the same experience as myself, but who, unlike me, may not have tried to conquer their nervousness.

What cured my fear was the purchase of a little shilling book called, I believe, 'Guide to Cycling', wherein it is written that cycles are 'vehicles within the meaning of the Act'. I then realised that I had an actual legal existence on the roadway, that my death by lawless violence would be avenged and that I was not, what I had hitherto felt myself to be, like the lady, hated both of gods and men, who "cast the golden fruit upon the board[57]" – I mean, my cycle on the streets – "and bred this change". Yes, I had as good a right to my life as even my arch-enemy the hansom, or my treacherous companion the butcher's cart. I and my machine were no longer like a masterless dog and if we were scouted from the pavement, at least we would take modestly but firmly, if need be, our proper breathing room in the road. From this moment my attitude towards hansoms was, in the classic words of 'Punch', *"Also schnapp ich meine finger in deinem face"*. Cautious and alert, I merrily proceeded on my way, using my bicycle as a means of doing my morning shopping or other business. I found that my experience in driving an exceedingly naughty pony in a cart in town stood me here in very good stead, my eye being fairly educated to pace and distance; and soon I learnt to judge of the breadth of my handle-bars almost to an inch and of the habits and probable proceedings of the various vehicles by which I was surrounded, with nothing, apparently, but my wits and nerve between me and destruction.

Drivers of hansoms have various ways of inflicting torture on a fellow-creature, one of which is suddenly and loudly to shout out 'Hi!' when they have ample room to pass, or when you are only occupying your lawful position in a string of vehicles. Also, they love to share your handle-bars and wheels, passing so close that if you swerve in the slightest – which, if you are possessed of nerves, you are likely to do – it must bring you to serious grief. They are also fond of cutting in just in front of you, or deliberately checking you at a crossing, well knowing that by so doing they risk your life, or, at any rate, force you to get off.

I myself always ride peaceably about seven or eight miles an hour, and keep a good look-out some way ahead, as by that means you can often slip through a tight place or avoid being made into a sandwich composed of, let us say, a pedestrian who will not and an omnibus which cannot, stop. As regards the comparative demerits of omnibuses and hansoms, I am reminded of the old riddle, 'Why have white sheep more wool than black ones?' The answer is 'Because there are more of 'em!' But not only are omnibuses fewer in number, but the drivers thereof are very *bons princes*; and, as they are great, so are they merciful. We ladies are not the kind of game at which they fly; for, although we are told that the inside places in these conveyances are all filled by countesses and

---

[57] Eris, goddess of discord, in Tennyson's 'The Death of Œnone'

duchesses nowadays, while the outside is covered by the younger members of their families, the aristocratic votaries of the wheel are in too small a minority to occasion the companies any anxiety except as to the social *ton* of their venture.

Many a time when I first began to ride in traffic have I meekly escorted an omnibus in a crowded thoroughfare, thankful for the shelter it afforded from the wild and skirmishing jungle round me and feeling like what I may perhaps describe as a dolphin playing round an ocean liner. Many acts of courtesy have I received at difficult crossings from hard-worked men, to whom pulling up their horses must have been a serious inconvenience. Indeed, on one occasion, I might have been killed but for the consideration of a driver. In trying to turn into Sloane Street from Knightsbridge I found myself wedged in between an omnibus and a large van, the former going down, the latter coming up, on opposite sides of that very narrow piece of road. They had both been standing and at the moment of my appearance each pulled out from the kerb in a slanting direction. I was thus fairly caught in a trap, as I had already turned the corner; but, not having time to faint or go into hysterics, I thought it best to catch the nearest omnibus horse by the bit and try to stop him. I cannot think now how I contrived to do this without a fall; but, in all the confusion of the moment, I distinctly recollect sitting on my bicycle, holding the horse's head, and turning round to thank the driver for checking his restive team while I got away unhurt.

My life was safe, it is true; but what is life if your new white gloves are ruined? Such, alas! was my melancholy condition and all because omnibus companies will not pay proper attention to the cleaning of bits. I had not the heart to reproach the driver, who, after all, like the American pianist, had done his best; but I felt like a friend of mine, who was ship-wrecked off the coast of Mull and who, when I offered him my warmest congratulations on not being drowned, replied in these words: "Yes, it was rather a nuisance. I lost a favourite paper-cutter and, what's more, got my boots wet". Be this as it may, I have avoided the turning from Knightsbridge into Sloane Street ever since. It is one of the most dangerous in London, not excepting the three circuses – Piccadilly, Regent or Oxford – where, at least, people are on the *qui vive* and are looking out for squalls from all points of the compass.

To my mind the great accomplishment for the cyclist in traffic is to be able to ride steadily, without too much wavering of his front wheel, at a very slow pace, so as to avoid getting off and then with quick eye and judgment to make a dash where he sees his opportunity, never forgetting to look some distance ahead so as to avoid stoppages. In these cases, like all others, prevention is better than cure.

Another word I should like to say. For riding in the streets it is most essential to have one hand free and therefore to be able to guide your bicycle with one hand; but acrobatic performances, such as riding without using either hands or feet down inclines in crowded streets, or with both feet on one side, or with your face to the hind wheel, as one man managed to do, are entirely to be discouraged. How

234

I admired at first the graceful way in which a gentleman, very tall and well known in royal social circles, took off his hat and bowed to his acquaintance on the pavement! I even envied the more humble individual whom I saw blowing his nose with reckless violence in Piccadilly; but now it seems to me that to fall would be impossible, even if I tried and this is really the only frame of mind in which it is safe to bicycle in the streets of London.

(The Badminton Magazine, 1896)

Whizz Kid

(1898)
Bicycle Riding – a Threat to Women's Health, Morals, and Reputation

The advent of the bicycle in the 1880s stimulated great controversy about women's proper role in society. Questions of 'how they should ride, when they should ride, who they should ride with' were considered by commentators and 'wheelings'. Many critics were certain that bicycle riding threatened women's health, morals, and reputation. Critics opposed wearing union suits (to absorb perspiration) or bloomers and worried about the privacy and potential liberty bicycling granted to young men and women. Physicians Thomas Lothrop and William Potter posited that the bicycle inevitably promoted immodesty in women and could potentially harm their reproductive systems. Other critics argued that women bicyclists favoured shorter skirts, thus 'inviting' insults and advances. Moreover, by tilting the bicycle seat, they could 'beget or foster the habit of masturbation'. For advocates like Maria E. Ward, however, the bicycle (was) an educational factor creating the desire for progress, the preference for what is better, the striving for the best, broadening the intelligence and intensifying love of home and country.

Before such noble attributes could be encouraged by 'the wheel', change in dress or the design of bicycles was necessary. Skirts made riding the Ordinary (a bicycle with a large front wheel) virtually impossible. Tricycles, however, were designed to accommodate full skirts and allowed women to ride without adopting the bloomer outfit, which many women opposed for its politically radical associations. Like nearly every other aspect of life in the nineteenth century, tricycle riding had a specific set of rules and regulations. The rule against women riding alone in fact generated a new profession: the professional lady cyclist as chaperone. Tricycles were commonly used for touring and the tandem tricycle was popular with couples.

The first bicycle with two equal-size wheels and a dropped frame with no crossbar was the Victor, first manufactured in 1887. With the addition of pneumatic tyres (invented in 1889[58]) and enclosed gear, women were able to ride comfortably without their skirts becoming entangled. The final dramatic improvement in bicycle technology was the coaster brake, invented in 1898. These features enabled women to bicycle safely without having to wear bloomers.

By 1900 bicycle manufacturers, sales agencies and private individuals had opened women's velocipede or riding schools in many north-eastern [American] cities. The Metropolitan Academy in New York City set aside a special area of its hall for women wishing to learn the mysteries of wheeling and installed the first athletics-linked shower baths for women in America. The Michaux Club, a New York City organization founded in 1895, provided women with riding lessons in the morning, music to accompany indoor riding after lunch and afternoon tea in the clubroom. The club also provided 'ten pin rides' in which women demonstrated their skill by riding slalom-fashion through lines of bowling pins set on the floor. Indoor riding for women was more acceptable to critics than outdoor bicycling because it was controlled; there was neither the possibility of young couples riding off in private, nor any chance of immodest exposure of women's limbs. Men were excluded from the women's bicycling sessions.

By the late 1880s two or three day tours under the aegis of regional or national cycling groups were common middle class activities. In both Europe and America these organizations charged small membership fees and issued road books which provided information about routes, road conditions, hotels, repair shops, and

---

[58] Actually invented and patented in 1846; first produced commercially in 1888

'consuls' – club members in towns and cities, appointed to answer the questions of touring cyclists. Far fewer women than men belonged to these groups, but they evidently participated with equal enthusiasm. In 1888 the Philadelphia Tricyclists Club had 118 members, eighteen of whom were women. That year the club's 'Captain's Cup', annually awarded to the member who covered the most miles during the year, was won by a woman 'for her mileage record of 3,304 ¼ miles'.

(Victorian Entertainment, vicfun.blogspot.com)

ROUTLEDGE'S 'EVERY BOY'S ANNUAL' (1870)

Velocipedes

Whether velocipedes will ever become a necessity of our civilization – the 'fast' adjunct to our 'fast' age – it is impossible to say, though appearances would warrant such a prediction. There are enthusiasts who see in a bicycle the solution of some gnarled social problem and believe that a tricycle will obviate some festering evil of our era, though at present the popular toy of the hour only flatters our pride by giving power over space; and there are those who sneer at the new-fangled contrivances and point out that similar machines have been used before and found woefully wanting. They predict ruptures, sprains, dislocation and death as the penalty of using these mechanical contrivances. They point out that they are excessively laborious to work, that there are a thousand abstract arguments why they cannot succeed; and whilst they are proving the case velocipedes are to be found in our streets, and our gymnasiums are thronged by anxious learners and expectant possessors of the new iron horse and carriage combined.

If the velocipedes of today were of the same construction as those which belonged to the past, no reasonable individual could deny that their use involved danger and fatigue without any compensation whatever, for those who tried them found that, though they succeeded in a certain sense, yet the result was so meagre as to furnish a familiar exemplification of 'the work not being worth the candle'. The principle was present in the old hobbyhorse, but the power was misapplied, and hence the failure and abandonment of the idea of making the velocipede popular. The shaking, squeaking three or four wheel spasmodic machines were discarded and placed in the same category as flying machines and perpetual motion.

Until the past few months it was always understood that velocipedes were invented about the year 1819, but recently one daring writer has asserted that the idea was coeval with the invention of the crank, which, after all, gives no higher antiquity, for, strange to say, the simplest of all inventions for turning a vertical into a rotary motion is not so old as the century.

The Parisians, who have the honour of resuscitating and making velocipedes fashionable and yet popular, claim the honour also of its invention. They point to the *Journal de Paris* of July 27, 1779, which describes a vehicle invented by the celebrated aeronaut M. Blanchard, in connection with M. Masurier. As far as can be judged from the description, this machine was a combination of the hobbyhorse and trolley: one man was seated in front and acted as driver or guide, whilst another supplied the motive power by pressing his feet alternately on the ground. This individual must have had a hard time of it, for it was found exhausting work to move the old velocipedes by the same means, though the weight could not have been more than a third of M. Blanchard's machine and driver. It is thought (for there is little known positively on the subject) that the manual power was aided by some mechanical contrivances, of which springs formed a part. This invention was exhibited both at Paris and Versailles, but it does not appear to have met with either royal or popular favour.

A generation later the *célérifère* made its appearance in the gardens of the Luxembourg; but, from the caricatures, it was evidently but a clumsy variation of the old hobbyhorse, with its low wheels and rupture producing movements. We, who are familiar with the controlling power and automatic movements of the modern bicycle, can hardly realize the formidable difficulties of this unmanageable and barbarous contrivance. It was propelled by the action of the feet on the ground; there were no means of guiding, controlling, or directing its movements; whilst an unfortunate slip or false movement resulted in painful sprains.

A dozen years afterwards, and we enter into the regular historic period of velocipedes and find them in use in England. At first they consisted simply of two wheels, very similar to the present bicycles in appearance, but were propelled by the action of the feet on the ground. The following is a sketch of one of these hobbyhorse contrivances, sketched more than thirty years ago. One somewhat similar in construction was used for many years by one of the Northamptonshire peasants, but the wheels were of less diameter. A drawing of an American one of the same period shows that the general principle was the same throughout, though varied in form and construction.

The Old Hobby-Horse

239

The next machines that came on the scene are hardly yet displaced by the Parisian and American improvements. We have seen them used in a fashionable town within the year.

They were three and four wheeled vehicles, moved by a series of treadles and levers, acting on cranks. They never were, or could be, popular; for a man could walk a dozen miles with twice the ease he could propel himself along in the old-fashioned velocipede.

The modern bicycle or horse-carriage is a very different contrivance. By exercise of the same exertion as he would use in walking a dozen miles he can travel thirty at least on an average road. This is denied by some sceptical theorists, but there is no valid reason to doubt the fact. Every step of the treadle, instead of carrying the body forward thirty inches, carries the vehicle forward three yards, and we are not surprised to learn that twelve miles an hour is a common speed for an expert, or that a mile has been 'done' in a race in less than four minutes.

The rage for velocipedes has been so great and so universal in Paris that nobles and commoners have vied with each other in the completeness and elegance of their equipment. Periodic races take place, and many of the riders display the utmost dexterity on their fragile and dangerous-looking vehicles. Government officials and mechanics use them in going to and from their employment and even the Prince Imperial[59] has been furnished with an elegant velocipede of rosewood and aluminium bronze. The prices of the Paris vehicles range from fifty francs for one suited for a boy, to two hundred francs and upwards, according to the style and finish.

The idea of annihilating space seems to have tickled the American fancy quite as much as the French. Their riding-schools are nightly thronged by hundreds who wish to acquire this new method of locomotion. We even learn that one of the Fifth Avenue art-galleries in New York has been converted into a velocipede riding-school. Not only is there a great want of accommodation to practise, but the manufacturers cannot produce velocipedes fast enough to supply the demand. The French pattern has been considerably modified by the Americans, but the singularly high price for so simple-looking a piece of workmanship has been maintained. The price of a plain substantial machine is $100, and those which are sumptuously fitted with ivory handles and silver plating have fetched $200. This high price is attributed to the number of skilled artisans employed in their construction and to the fact that nothing but the very best of material can be used. Every piece must be made by hand, of wrought iron, steel, or brass. It is as well to state that cast iron has been used and discarded as dangerous to the rider and pecuniarily fatal to the manufacturer. The patterns of the velocipedes most in vogue are the Wood, Pickering, and Hanlon machines, all varying in some small detail from the French pattern. Of these it is estimated that 5,000 will be in use by

---

[59] Son of Napoleon III

the course of the summer in New York and its vicinity alone. The demand is so great that some of the leading carriage-builders have devoted a large portion of their establishments to this branch of business. They, however, pay a royalty to Mr Calvin Witty, who, seeing that velocipedes were likely to prove a 'big thing', secured the patent in the United States for bicycles, to the disgust of the other manufacturers.

In Great Britain the movement has brought out the old four-wheeled velocipede, which is so little under control that a poor woman lost her life through one in Glasgow this year. We have before us, however, the designs for at least five-and-twenty varieties of bicycles and tricycles, the result of British ingenuity. Some of these are the perfection of absurdity and those which are immediately and essentially practical are advertised at prices which seem preposterous considering the simplicity of their construction. The lowest sum that we have heard asked for a bicycle is £8, and at first sight it seems that half that sum would be ample, as the wheels alone can be purchased retail at 30s the pair. But skilled workmen are scarce and the various manufactories engaged in making the new wheel-horse are so busy that until the demand slackens no material reduction in price may be looked for. Mr Lisle, of Wolverhampton, has, however, advertised a variety of bicycles and tricycles at a price so moderate that they deserve the attention of every intending purchaser. The patterns are the very best and most approved construction. He has the French, American, and German patterns of bicycles, and his tricycles, especially those adapted for ladies, are models of beauty and strength. We intend in a future paper to give engravings of bicycles and tricycles together with the most explicit directions as to making and using velocipedes, so that young gentlemen can have them made of a size to fit their height and other peculiarities. We may add that about twenty hours' practice is all that is necessary to give facility and adroitness in balancing and managing a bicycle.

The Bicycle

It would have been a slur on the mechanical genius of a manufacturing age if no machine could be invented to enable man to have quicker, easier, and safer modes of transit than those which depend on expensive appliances and combination of labour and capital, or those which rely on animal assistance. Some of our best machines are the simplest and inventors have too frequently erred by using complicated movements when the simple ones were within their grasp and far better adapted for their purpose. Thus it is said that Watt devised a thousand schemes for turning a vertical into a rotary or a horizontal one, but did not think of the crank. The simplicity of the dandy-horse, or, as we should term it, the Von Drais velocipede, was all that could be desired, but it unfortunately did not utilize the power of man. The extra speed was gained at a vast expense of power. The wheel-horse of that day was not under control – it was crude. It wanted the crank, and unfortunately for the enthusiastic velocipedist, it was not adapted to it. When cranks were used they were adapted to a four or three-wheeled carriage, with

241

what success I have shown. Cogs, pinions, cranks, wheels within wheels, and all mechanical contrivances to gain power did so at the expense of speed; and though many of the contrivances are admirably adapted to enable invalids to move themselves about in a Bath chair – nay are even now manufactured for that purpose – nevertheless for speed the power must be applied direct, and how this has been accomplished a glance at the American patent records will speedily show us.

First in point of time was the 'Cantering Propeller', invented by Mr P. W. Mackenzie, a citizen of the United States, who in 1862 patented in America an automatic horse (Fig. 1), and has since reissued the patent with a view, evidently, of covering the whole ground of American manufacture now in dispute between Messrs Witty and Smith for the Lambelle[60] principle. The claim has been reissued in the following terms:

Fig. 1 – The Cantering Propeller

1. I claim in combination with a saddle seat for the rider, the employment and use of a cranked axle, arms, and foot-rest, so arranged that the power applied by the feet of the rider shall give motion to the vehicle, substantially as described and specified.

2. The combination of the following elements: namely, a saddle seat for the rider, a cranked axle for propelling the vehicle by power applied by the feet of the rider, and a steering mechanism, so constructed that the direction of travel of the vehicle may be governed by the rider, substantially as described and specified.

---

[60] Possibly an error for Lallement

242

3. The universal joint, in combination with the fulcrum of the vehicle and the steering wheel, constructed and operating substantially as and for the purposes specified.

4. The hinged legs in combination with the body of the horse and with the cranks, substantially as and for the purposes specified.

5. The foot-rests upon the arm, substantially as and for the purposes specified.

6. The double-armed levers and diagonal cords in combination with the handle and steering-wheel, substantially as described and specified.

There is no doubt that this claim embraces all the essential points of the modern bicycle.

A Monsieur Rivière describes in the patent journals his improvement on the old dandy-horse. He fixed the axle of the front wheel so that it rotated with the wheel itself, and passed through headings formed in the vertical steering-fork of the vehicle, and each end of the axle was provided with a crank having a balance foot-plate, so that the rider could give motion to the machine through the cranked axle which actuated the front wheel, instead of pressing his feet against the ground as in the old arrangement. This is the exact arrangement of the modern bicycle driving-wheel. He also points out: "In constructing a velocipede according to this invention, I prefer that the seat or saddle should be supported by a spring, and that a cross handle should be provided for actuating the vertical steering-fork of the front wheel, such cross handle being connected by a strap to one end of a lever of the first order, having its fulcrum in the main beam of the vehicle, and the lever being so arranged that by partially rotating the cross handle upon its axis the front end of the lever is drawn up, and its lower end simultaneously actuates a spring brake, which is pressed against the periphery of the back wheel of the velocipede, thus retarding its motion as desired. When not required to be used, the lever is kept out of action by a spring provided for that purpose. The two wheels must be in a line with each other, and I prefer that the front wheel should be somewhat larger in diameter than the back one." Had M. Rivière completed his specification, and added the necessary drawings, he would have been the patentee of the bicycle. Whether he was the inventor, or whether he had previously seen the French or American bicycle, we have no means of knowing.

Thus, like many useful inventors, the real inventor of the modern bicycle is open to grave doubt. The simplest form, and the easiest made by amateurs, is shown in Fig. 2. If this velocipede was made with a brake, either self-acting, as in Fig. 5, or with a cord to the guide handles, it would be peculiarly well adapted for heavy men. It has the simplicity of the old dandy-horse with the power and improvements of the modern bicycle.

We are now face to face with the most popular form of the French bicycle (Fig. 3). The pattern is that made by Mr Lisle, of Moorfields, Wolverhampton. It is fitted with lamp and brake complete. The brake is worked by turning the guide-arms. It has all the essentials both in theory and in practice of a first class and useful velocipede.

Fig. 2 – The Bicycle

A very strong, popular and showy form of velocipede is that shown at Fig. 4. The brake can either be made self-acting or by the action of the French bicycle (Fig. 3) preceding. I have shown the triangular reel-treadles in place of the weighted slipper.

Fig. 3 – The French Bicycle
The iron frame on the hind wheel, or a brake may be placed as shown in Fig. 4.

244

Fig. 4 – The Parisian Bicycle

When the bicycle reached America, the various manufacturers introduced improvement and varieties of patterns. The pattern known in America as Pickering's (Fig. 5) has become known and popular in England as the American bicycle. The saddle is supported on a spiral spring, and fitted with a self-acting brake beneath.

Fig. 5 – The American Bicycle

The patentees claim for this pattern great credit. They affirm that it is simpler, more durable, lighter, stronger, and cheaper than either of the French patterns. The great feature of difference is, however, the connecting apparatus. In this the saddle-bar serves not only as a seat but as a brake, and is not attached to the rear wheel. By a simple pressure forward against the tiller, and a backward pressure against the tail of the saddle, the saddle-spring is compressed, and the brake attached to it brought firmly down upon the wheel.

Another of the American patterns is the one introduced by Hanlon Brothers (Fig. 6), and known by their name.

Fig. 6 – The Hanlon Velocipede

In this the extending or slipping crank for the pedal was made a feature. The bearings of the guide-fork admit of easy lubrication and cleaning. The saddle is placed on a spring of wood or metal. Its great drawback is the want of a brake. It has met with little favour in England, though its simplicity and strength deserve a favourable consideration.

There have been some modifications of the bicycle patented. One notably, by Mr W. E. P. Gibbs, of London, in which the hind wheel is driven by cranks, whilst the front wheel is very small and is simply used for the purpose of guiding the vehicle. The experience of all velocipedists points to a large driving-wheel in front as the best and easiest to work.

The American papers mention the invention of a velocipede of an entirely new style, called the 'Keystone', invented by Professor Lowback of Philadelphia and so named by him in honour of his native state. It has but two wheels and the seat is quite low between them. The novelty consists in a cog attached to the guiding-post by means of which the rear-wheel is made to follow directly in the track of the driving-wheel. The description is not very explicit; but we are further told that no matter how short the curve, both wheels make it at the same time and the seat always remains parallel to the driving-wheel. In the other machines there is no guide to the rear wheel and consequently the machine cannot be turned so readily when a collision is threatened. In practice, however, this alleged drawback does not exist, as the French bicycle can be turned round almost in its own length. In a room or riding-school no doubt the 'Keystone' would be useful.

246

The Tricycle

In all probability the three-wheeled velocipede will have a more enduring and wider-spread popularity than the two-wheeled. Not that those in present use are safer or even easier to guide than the bicycle, but they permit the body to remain in a sitting posture when going down hill and when the machine is at rest. An artist can sketch from the seat. It can be taken to a shady nook while the luncheon or quiet pipe is enjoyed and what is lost in speed is made up in comfort. There, are, however, some drawbacks. Strange as it may appear to the uninitiated, the tricycle is far more likely to upset the tyro than the bicycle. Some modifications in the form of the machine have been made which bid fair to remove this objection.

The simplest form of a tricycle is shown in Fig. 7. It is one of those manufactured by Mr Lisle, of Wolverhampton, and is known as the German tricycle. It is, in fact, a converted bicycle of the American pattern. The rear wheel is removed and its place supplied by a pair of wheels running free on an axle two feet long. The motive power is supplied by the crank pedals attached to the front axle. There is not much loss of power in this form of bicycle, but there is a tendency to turn over when the machine is not running on the crown of the road.

Fig. 7 – The German Tricycle

The Americans cling pertinaciously to the direct action principle and whilst they have recognised the disabilities under which the bicycle labours, they have endeavoured to overcome these blemishes without reverting to the treadle and lever. A machine has been invented by Messrs Topliff & Ely, of Elyria, Ohio, which attempts to combine the advantages of both the bicycle and the tricycle, by means of a depressed V axle to the rear wheels. This axle, by means of a lever, enables the rider at will to change the distance between the hind wheels from two feet to two inches or less, so that he can practise in the beginning on the three wheels, and as he gains confidence can change the machine practically into a bicycle. Fig. 8 shows a perspective elevation of this machine, with diagrams showing the action of the rear wheels. They may be made to run on any portion of the axle, and are prevented from coming together by the fixed collar at B. The lever for turning the axle is shown at A.

Fig. 8 – The Elyria Velocipede

Recent numbers of the *Scientific American* contain the drawing of a tricycle, which has many advantages to recommend it (Fig. 9). It was designed by Mr John Tremper, of Wilmington, in the United States. It has the driving-wheel in front, with the direct action of the reel pedals, but the wheel is placed much nearer to the rear wheels than any of the tricycles yet made. This gives the rider a more complete control over the motion and action of the machine and enables it to turn corners with the safety and celerity of the two-wheeler. Its construction is thus described:

From the axle of the hind wheel rises a bow-shaped brace, to which is bolted one end of the reach, which consists of two parallel pieces of wood bolted together, and embracing between them an upright standard or pipe, terminating in a forked brace, in which the driving-wheel turns, and having directly over the wheel's rim, where the forked braces unite, a brake-shoe or pad. The weight on the driving-wheel and part of that of the rider are sustained by a spiral spring, as seen in the woodcut, which serves as a buffer in passing over irregularities of the ground. The steering-bar, which is a prolongation of the forked brace, passes up through the hollow standard, and is furnished with handles, as usual, at the top. The seat, or saddle, is sustained by two cast steel springs, secured to the front of the reach by means of a cross strap, or block and bolt, so that it is easily adjusted further to the front or rear, as may be desired. The upright tube may also be adjusted in the reach to suit the length of legs or arms of the rider.

Fig. 9 – The Wilmington Tricycle

Fig. 10 – Lisle's Ladies' English Velocipede

Some of the points in this machine are well worth the careful consideration of the velocipede manufacturer. A leg-rest would improve it. Its good qualities would recommend it on fair roads; indeed the great, if not its only drawback, is the width of the hind wheels apart, which would prevent the rider from picking his road with the ease he does on the bicycle. Several modifications have been proposed,

249

but none of the machines using the front wheel as a driving-wheel differ materially in form or construction from those delineated.

The tricycle, when fitted with a seat instead of a saddle, became a favourite with the fair sex of Paris. The necessity of the case suggested many modifications in the construction of the machine. The front wheel is only used for steering purposes and as a support to the reach. The power is supplied by treadles and levers, acting on cranks in the axle of the rear wheels. The seat is a cushion chair of horsehair and wicker-work, fixed between the hind wheels and supported by the reach and bearings on the axles. Mr Lisle's 'Ladies' English Velocipede' (Fig. 10) furnishes a good pattern of this elegant vehicle.

The downward curve of the reach in this pattern does away with the objection to the Parisian tricycle (Fig. 11), in which the reach is either straight and suggestive of an ungraceful attitude, or curved sideways, which is emblematic of weakness.

The pedals are furnished with slipper-shaped rests for the feet, and are so formed as to enable the rider to disengage her foot instantly. The motive power is similar to that of weaving and is analogous to walking. There is no pressure of the foot, and the leg is fully extended without any cramping effort. Some of the larger and more powerful velocipedes of this principle (see Fig. 11) are fitted with side levers, which act on the cranked axle and materially increase the speed, and at the same time serve, if necessary, as a brake, by the rider pressing against it. The steering handle is fixed like that of an ordinary Bath chair.

Fig. 11 – Ladies' Parisian Tricycle

250

Since the recent revival of the velocipede movement there have been many suggestive improvements, but there are none which increase the power. A favourite notion is the use of direct foot motion on the cranked knee or toggle joint; and the other the use of a fixed straight lever acting in the same manner by the weight of the body. I have seen three-wheeled velocipedes with the two driving-wheels in front, attached to a triangular frame; but neither the rider nor the lookers-on pronounced it a success. There was some difficulty in steering it, and it had an inherent disposition to travel backwards. Except for ladies, the treadle machines offer no advantages. They afford healthful exercise to the fair sex and, on comparatively level ground, they would doubtless be found an agreeable adjunct to a country life.

In many fashionable spas, Bath chairs, furnished with a handle and multiplying-wheels, are frequently seen, in which invalids can move themselves about. They are an admirable contrivance for exercise, but their speed is that of the tortoise, not of the hare. The 'Ransome' velocipede of Messrs Ransome is a modification of a tricycle, with levers and treadles.

Four-wheelers

No description of velocipedes would be perfect without some allusion to the favourite 'four-wheeler' of the past generation of mechanics. The idea of the four-wheeler is perfect security, space for a companion, and an imposing appearance. The drawbacks are want of control, steering-brakes, loss of power, and expense. There are numberless varieties and patterns of these machines, all of which have their admirers. Amongst the best, if not the very best, is one manufactured by Mr Andrews, of Dublin, the construction of which will be best understood by reference to Figs. 12 and 13.

The frame of this velocipede is made of the best inch-square iron, seven feet long between perpendiculars. The treadles are made of the best ash, 1½ inch by 1¼ inch, 6 feet 6 inches long. The wheels should be made as the best velocipede wheels are made, of elm stocks, 4 inches by 5 inches; hickory spokes, which should not exceed 7/8 inch by 3/4 inch, tapering to 3/4 inch to 1/2 inch. The felloes are made of best ash, bent in one piece, so that they only require one joining; light steel tires. Mr Andrews makes his wheels 3 feet 4 inches high; but if similar wheels are made for a bicycle, they should not exceed 32 or 34 inches high.

The fore wheels move freely on an axle, which is fixed by a pivot to the reach or frame and a steering-handle is likewise attached to the axle by a lever brace. The reach is curved upwards, to support a cross bar on which the treadles are suspended: it is forked under the seat, and lies over the cranked axle on brass bearings. The seat should be made as light as possible, of some wicker or cane work and may be stuffed with hair.

This form of velocipede admits of hand-levers being fitted, as shown by the dotted lines, Fig. 12. The other dotted lines show the positions for a valise, box, or portmanteau at the back of the seat or above the front axle.

Fig. 12 – The Dublin Velocipede

Mr Sawyer, of Dover, is another well-known maker of four-wheelers. One of the most recent suggestions for the improvement of this class of velocipedes is to gain additional power by dispensing with the treadles and permit the feet to work directly on knee-joints in the axle of the front wheels. This plan does not overcome the objections that have been raised to the four-wheelers in general.

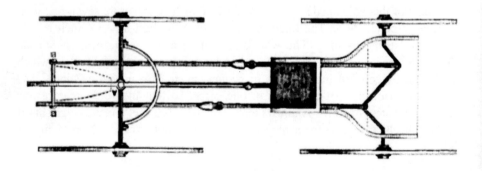

Fig. 13 – The Dublin Four-wheeler

The Art of Velocipede Management

As in most other accomplishments, practice alone can make a skilful rider of velocipedes. The tyro can, however, profit by the experience of others, and I give a few rules for his guidance, as well as directions for his practice. The first point is to gain confidence in, and familiarity with, his wheel horse. If he has had one made according to the directions here given, he will know its parts and proportions intimately. If he has but recently purchased one, he should walk by its side, guiding it by the handle until he knows its movements thoroughly. He will see that it obeys, almost like a 'thing of life', the slightest movement of the handle, and follows the driving-wheel in all its tortuous movements.

The second step of progress is to gain and keep the balance when astride on the saddle. This is apparently a very difficult feat to accomplish, but really it is not so. After sitting for a few minutes in the velocipede, with the toes touching the ground, the vehicle may be placed on a slight incline, so that it may run down of its own accord. The handle must be gripped firmly and steadily, and the feet just lifted from the ground. If there is a disposition to swerve either to the right or left, in consequence of the inclination of the body disturbing the equilibrium, a slight alteration of the pressure on the handle will restore the lost balance. In the riding-schools it is usual for the assistant to steady the velocipede in the earlier lessons; but, like learning to swim on corks, it is far better to dispense with this extraneous aid, so that the rider may study the action of the machine himself. He will find the sensation peculiar at first, but a slight practice will habituate him to it. At first he will wish the handles were firmer, for each nervous twist that he gives it as the machine moves is calculated either to upset his balance or to turn the vehicle out of a straight line.

A few runs down an incline will pave the way for the first real lesson on self-propulsion. At first, it will be better to lift each leg alternately, so that they may follow the movement of the pedal without exerting any force. This will habituate the knees and feet to the movement. It is during this practice that the arm of a friend or the ready hand of a skilled assistant is valuable, as there is always a disposition to press too hardly on the pedal. It does not require the strength of an elephant to turn the driving-wheel, even on the roughest road; and in these preliminary trials it is quite unnecessary. The engraving (Fig. 14) 'The Mount' shows the position of starting. Observe the position of the pedal, on which the left leg is resting.

It is placed in such a position that the mere weight of the rider will cause the machine to move. Ere he has brought the foot down, his right leg will find a resting-place on the corresponding pedal, and by the exercise of a little downward pressure alternately as each pedal turns, progress will be made, as shown in Fig. 15 and Fig. 16.

Fig. 14 – The Mount

Fig. 15 – The Start. Just off

254

It is very important that the pedals should be placed at the angle indicated, as it gives the necessary impetus to the start. Should there be any danger of falling, take the foot off the pedals on the side and rest it on the ground, and commence afresh. It is by no means uncommon for the learner to be able to run a distance of fifty or sixty yards after a few hours' practice. To alight it is only necessary to apply the brake by turning the handle. To slacken the speed, release the feet from the pedals and place them simultaneously on the ground.

In all the earlier essays choose some unfrequented road for practice, and avoid as far as possible a crowded thoroughfare.

Practise at first down hill; the use of the brake will at all times prevent excessive speed. Beware of advancing vehicles and abrupt crossing of roads. Do not ride on the foot-paths!

When practice has given a tolerable command over the vehicle (and a young, active man will acquire that command in a fortnight's practice of a couple of hours a day), the legs may be elevated to the rest when the velocipede descends a hill, so that it may run free. The preliminary position of doing this is shown in Fig. 16. The right leg is raised on to the cross rest beneath the angle, whilst the hands firmly grasp the handle.

Fig. 16 – Preparing to go down hill

A slight effort will raise the left leg to the other side of the rest (Fig. 17). The velocipede will run now down hill by its own gravitation, whilst the rider controls its movements by the aid of the brake. It requires but little practice to perform this feat adroitly, in fact, the greater the speed the more perfect the balance.

In all early efforts the ascent of a hill should be avoided. It is very discouraging to the learner, and causes him to lose confidence in himself and his vehicle. When perfect command is obtained over the velocipede, comparatively steep hills maybe ascended without much difficulty. Old velocipedists all affirm that it is better and wiser on long journeys to walk up the hills, for there is a much less expenditure of power in walking up the hills and leading the bicycle, or even pushing a four-wheeler, than in attempting to force it along by means of the treadles.

With respect to the command over the velocipede, I have seen comparative beginners in the course of a month's practice describe a series of circles or a figure of eight with ease. It is by no means impossible to turn a circle at full speed a little more in diameter than the length of the machine itself.

Fig. 17 – Off down hill

One of the objections made to the use of the bicycle is that a slight impediment would cause it to overturn; but practically this is not the case. A recent velocipede steeplechase at the gymnasium at Liverpool showed that the bicycle could perform wonders, going easily over large thick mats and planks spread about without upsetting the riders; as many as three mats were cleared at one time in excellent style. During this race Mr Shepherd, one of the velocipedists, mounted on to the narrow seat and balanced himself on one foot whilst the bicycle was going at a rapid rate. The vehicles used were the strong iron ones manufactured by Mr Brown of Liverpool.

256

How to construct a bicycle

However popular and however common velocipedes may become there will always remain a large section of the people to whom they will be and must be inaccessible in consequence of their price. At first sight there seems no reason why so large a sum should be charged for them. The lowest price quoted, as far as I have seen, was 35s for a tricycle adapted for rural postmen by Mr Lisle of Wolverhampton. For a well-built bicycle the lowest price yet quoted is £7 7s, though the advertised prices range from £10 to £20. Bicycles have been sold in America as high as 200 dollars with ivory handles and ornamental plating of silver. In Paris they are sold at all prices, from 200 to 400 francs. Velocipedes deluxe, such as that presented to the Prince Imperial, mount up to any sum, according to the amount of rosewood, carving, and aluminium bronze used.

Then there are numerous etceteras sold. Valise, lantern, oil-bottle, or grease-box, spanner in case of the machine getting out of order or India-rubber cushions for the iron cross-bar in front of the bicycle, on which the feet rest when going down hill. A cover, too, is wanted for the vehicle to preserve it from dust and some add an indicator to mark the distance travelled.

This sum is larger in consequence of the liability of the bicycle to rough usage and accidents. The best material must be used in the construction, or the result will be failure. Every piece must be made by hand of wrought iron, steel, or brass. Cast iron has been used and failed. It was dangerous to the rider, and pecuniarily fatal to the manufacturer. In large manufactories a variety of artisans are employed. One of the great American manufactories 'employs draughtsmen to design improvements, pattern-makers to prepare models for the foundry, blacksmiths to do the forging, wheelwrights for the wheels, machinists and fitters to turn and fit the various parts, foundry men to cast the pedals and traces, bolt makers to make the rivets and bolts, saddlers to prepare the seats and painters and varnishers to finish the machines for the ware-room'. Still it is possible for any ingenious mechanic to make one for himself if he attends to the dimensions and directions herewith given.

The Wheels

Wheels are of course the principal portion of the vehicle. They have been advertised at 30s the pair when made of iron. Good hickory wheels with steel tires cost more than that sum. The iron ones would probably prove as lasting.

The driving-wheel should never exceed 36 inches in diameter. An ordinary-sized man would find 30 inches high enough, for the pedals may be graduated on a slide to suit the length of leg and stride required. The height of the saddle should always admit of the feet being placed on the ground. This enables the rider to rest when tired in an easy position and gives him power to preserve himself from many an ugly tumble in the beginning of his career.

The dimensions of a full-sized French velocipede are various. If the driving-wheel is 36 inches in diameter the rear wheel should not exceed 32 inches and it is better to have two of 30 inches, so that it may be converted into a tricycle. The length between the centres should not exceed 44 inches. The rear wheels should run free on a fixed axle. The axle of the driving-wheel is either a part of the iron wheel, or keyed on to it, fitted with either square nuts or ornamental caps to keep the pedal-stays firmly in their places.

An exceedingly useful size, perhaps the most useful, is to have the driving-wheel 30 inches in diameter and the rear wheel 27 inches. The length between the centres would then be 30 inches.

Some additional strength is secured by placing the spokes on the nave stock alternately on one side and the other of the centre, as shown in Fig. 18. By far the cheapest plan is to buy a pair of tubular iron wheels. If, however, it is more handy to procure wooden wheels, the axle will have to be considered.

The Axle

The axle should be made of bar steel, one inch square, and keyed into the wooden nave with flat keys, or, what is better, a flat plate may be screwed on either side of the nave, with a square hole to fit the axle. The first inch of the axle outside the nave must be rounded to receive the fork. The next inch should be left square to receive the crank (Fig. 20), which may either be secured by an ordinary linch-pin as at A, Fig. 18, or by a screw and nut as at B. Another plan may be followed which has many advantages. The wheel may be left free on the axle as in an ordinary carriage, and on the outside of the nave a strong iron plate, Fig. 19, may be screwed, working with a ratchet-catch, B. The crank arm will then run free when descending an incline.

This modification is far better adapted for a treadle bicycle than for a bicycle, and can only be recommended when the nave of the wheel needs strengthening. As the rear wheel runs free on the axle, it may be secured by a simple nut and screw on each side of the reach fork, or by a linch-pin.

The Crank Shaft

The crank-shaft is shown at Fig. 20. The groove or slot enables the crank-pin bearing the pedal to be adjusted to any length required. It may be made of ⅜ inch iron. The groove or slot should be ⅜ inch wide and the width of the crank should be 1½ inch, as the strain is very great.

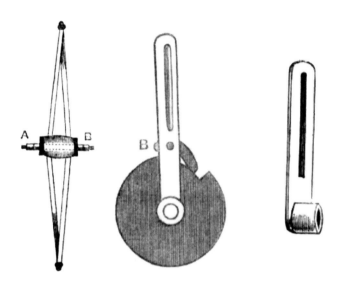

Fig. 18 – Nave stock, Fig. 19 – Iron plate, Fig. 20 – Crank

The Pedals

The pedals or stirrups are made of various shapes; those in the form of a slipper are now almost universally discarded in favour of the two varieties shown in Fig. 21. The first (A) is a three-sided wooden pedal with a circular brass flange turning freely on the crank-pin. The pressure of the foot will always bring one of the sides into proper position. They are so shaped as to allow of the use of the fore-part of the foot, bringing the ankle-joint into play, relieving the knee, and rendering propulsion much easier than when the shank of the foot is alone used, as in the slippers. The pattern B, which is weighted so as always to present the same surface to the foot, has many admirers. They are adjusted on the crank by means of a nut and screw. A plain crank-iron without a reel may be used.

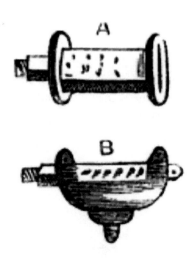

Fig. 21 – Pedals or stirrups

The Guide-fork or Brace

The guide-fork or brace is variously formed. The fork itself is half the diameter of the wheel, with sufficient play to let the latter run free. The bearing should be bushed with brass or composition metal. Thus, if the wheel is 30 inches high, the fork would have to be 16 inches, and the shaft 9 inches. It should be filed square at the top to secure the fork of the steering-handle, and the upper part tapped to receive a nut.

Fig. 22 – Guide-fork or Brace

The Steering Handle

The steering handle may be made of any fancy curve, a variety of which are shown in the engravings of the bicycles. A plain fork (Fig. 23) will answer every purpose of use and ornament. The shaft of the handles should have a hole drilled to receive the brake cord, if one is used, or an eyelet-hole may be welded on. The handles should be of wood.

Fig. 23 – Steering Handle

The Reach or Bearing-shaft

The reach or bearing-shaft is the most important portion of the whole, for unless it is of good material and well made, no possible satisfaction can be given. The simplest made and the cheapest is that shown in Fig. 24, but a handy smith would have but little difficulty in forming one similar to the Hanlon Velocipede (Fig. 6).

Fig. 24 – Reach or Bearing-shaft

A good stout ash bar is within the reach of every country and the majority of town lads; a cooper, joiner, or wheelwright (if the lad has no tools), would shape it into a form similar to Fig. 24. It should be some 4 feet long and 3 inches by two inches scantling. The bow carrying a collar, A, should be made of iron and screwed to the bearing-shaft to receive the guide-fork and a brass collar should be let into the shaft immediately beneath for the same purpose, as shown by dotted lines at B. The two supports to the hind wheel, one on each side, should be of a V shape, as in Fig. 25, so that they may be tightly screwed to the shaft. The arm might be lengthened at D on both sides, so that a pin or bolt could be inserted to support a steel spring for a saddle, the other end of which may be secured at C (Fig. 24).

The Saddle

The saddle may be supported on two spiral springs, or by eighteen inches of steel spring bolted through on the right side of the shaft at C, in the shape of Fig. 26. The saddle itself may be of wood, or stuffed with wool, and (Fig. 26) covered with leather or American cloth.

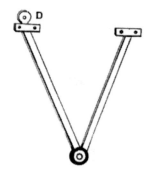

Fig. 25 – Supports to the hind wheel

Fig. 26 – Saddle

The Fitting

The fitting must next be considered. The brace-fork must be fitted on the driving wheel by screwing the caps to the flange and oiling it well. The crankshafts must follow at right angles to each other, and the nuts screwed tightly home. The bearing-shaft or reach should now be placed on the fork. Ere this is done, a collar of India-rubber, or a coil or two of spiral spring, should be placed over the outside of the fork, between it and the shaft, to act as a buffer. If neither India-rubber nor spring be handy, a few pieces of leather and cloth will be useful to prevent the jarring of the machine. The steering-handle may be fitted on and screwed down. It may require a few iron washers or rings to come firmly down to the collar; but this must not be screwed too tight. The V supports may now be secured in their places by bolts being run through the screw-holes and secured on the other side with nuts, so that the work will be exactly parallel. This is better than the plan shown in Fig. 2, of making the supports into forks, and bolting them through the wood. The first plan strengthens and the latter weakens the shaft. The rear wheel

262

may now be placed. A strong but simple steel bolt, with a linch-pin or nut, will answer for an axle. Fit on the saddle, and your velocipede is complete, with the exception of the brake, which is hardly necessary; but, if desired, it can be screwed beneath the shaft, so as to act on the hind wheel, as shown in Fig. 2. A piece of catgut, or even sash-cord, if knotted to the steering-handle and passed through a gimlet-hole in the shaft and attached to the end of the brake, will furnish sufficient power on the steering-handle being turned round. Fig. 27 shows the ordinary construction of a brake. It is made of iron, but the shaded part is wood, which will require renewing occasionally. Now you have a bicycle: ride, practise, and prosper.

Fig. 27 – Construction of a brake

Velocipedum Variorum

If one half of the suggestions which have been made for the use and improvement of velocipedes were turned to practical account, we should have air, earth, fire, and water vehicles in multifarious variety. Whether that famous six or seven wheeler, which is to carry a family party by a treadle movement, will ever become a reality it is difficult to say. The performance, to say the least of it, would be of a very cranky order. Wind velocipedes are nearly as old as the hills. They have been tried with flat and revolving sails, combining in the latter instance a land boat and a windmill, all of which are duly described in the 'Sailing-boat' by Mr H. C. Folkard and the results chronicled, even to the frightening of a farmer's wife and upsetting her in a ditch.

The marine velocipede, the podoscaphe, or *vélocipède marin,* which is the last new Parisian notion, has been tried for years with some success. Those on the lake of the Bois de Boulogne are 'formed of a couple of canoes covered with canvas and joined together by two iron bars, between which is a paddle-wheel, put in motion by means of two pedals placed at the extremity of the arc'. There was a talk that some enterprising gentleman would cross the Channel on one of these machines, but he has not yet done so. Some of the marine velocipedes suggested are manumotive machines, the movement of which is analogous to turning a mangle. Machines of this kind have been used for years without any great results being achieved.

Several suggestions have been made with respect to the application of steam to velocipedes. It might, and perhaps will be done; but then they will cease to be velocipedes. Read some of the latest ideas on the subject. The vehicle is to be constructed to carry two.

The means for working consists of a pair of oscillating cylinders, situated behind the carriage, driving a small cranked stage, having upon it the two driving-wheels. Steam is supplied from a small boiler, located in the front, and carried through the steam-pipe into the trunnion-box between the cylinders and after performing its work finds its passage into the exhaust-pipe in the usual manner. The exhaust-pipe is in connection with the funnel of the boiler, the latter being located underneath the carriage, so that no inconvenience may arise from smoke in front. The heat, too, from the boiler may all be avoided by placing around it some non-conducting material.

Fig. 28 – The application of steam to velocipedes

A handle where by the brake may be applied is in a convenient position and may be used to one or both wheels and the guide-wheel, worked by gearing, is so

264

placed that it may easily be handled by a passenger, who has the opportunity of transforming himself (for the time being) into an amateur engine-driver and stoker. Coals are carried in a bunker, situated in front of the boiler. The proposers and inventors may console themselves by knowing that in Mr Stuart's pleasant 'Anecdotes of the Steam-Engine', published forty years ago, there is a little vignette, a similar contrivance, of which Fig. 28 is a facsimile. The design seems to ridicule Messrs Baynes, Dumbell, Tindal, & Co. A reference to the 'Aids to Locomotion', issued by the Patent Office, will show that the idea dates at least from 1813.

The American Ice Velocipede (Fig. 29) is a much more sensible contrivance. It is literally skating by means of machinery. The design originally appeared in *Harper's Weekly* and the machine is intended to be used on ice or frozen snow. The driving-wheel is armed with sharp points to prevent the possibility of slipping, which proved so fatal to M. Dreuze's machine. The hind wheel is replaced by a pair of gigantic skates or runners, similar to those used in sleighs or ice-boats. It is hardly likely to have a fair trial in England.

This vehicle, with its one wheel, seems to have tickled the fancy of a Mr John St Leger Partridge, who has, or is, going to bring out the 'Victorine', or one-wheeled velocipede. *Bell's Life* informs the public, however, that this gentleman's labours in this direction have occupied the better portion of the last fourteen years. It is his intention, we are told, 'to test publicly the merits of his machine by an open trial'.

Fig. 29 – The American Ice Velocipede

To this end he issues a challenge to all comers to a race of velocipedes of any model, to some town not more than a hundred or less than fifty miles from

London. He further offers to give one mile start for every twenty in the course decided on, the road selected to be a fair average one as to ascents and descents. This 'sensation' match will doubtless be watched with much curiosity, as the Americans have attempted progression *en vélocipède* with positively one wheel. This Mr John St Leger Partridge must have taken a lesson out of Mr Dumbell's idea which is a spherical ball with compartments; or he must have adopted a squirrel-cage, or the clown's idea of riding on a barrel. The American idea is a combination of the two.

Far more useful and interesting are the various forms of a child's velocipede. The Prince Imperial, on the occasion of the Fête de Pâques, presented ten miniature velocipedes in aluminium bronze to his friends. The majority of the juvenile velocipedes are merely small varieties of those used by the seniors. There is, however, an adaptation of the 'cantering propeller' affixed to a tricycle, which combines the pleasure of a rocking-horse with actual progression. Such are a few of the many forms which velocipedes have assumed during the past fifteen months.

Progress of the Velocipede

La Belle France was the cradle of the velocipede. All that we know of its history points to France as its birthplace, and we are convinced now that its resuscitation is due to the *petits crevés* and *cocottes*[61] of Paris.

What a change from the cumbersome machine of M. Blanchard to the light and airy bicycle of the modern Parisian! But the change in popular opinion is even greater. It is true that caricaturists still make them the butt of their wit-pointed pencils; prince and peasant, noble and bourgeois – all vie with each other in their admiration of the new vehicle. A vivid account of the scene presented by the riders appears in the *London Society* for November. We are told that 123 miles have been accomplished within the twenty-four hours and that fifty miles in five hours have been repeatedly accomplished. Those who witnessed the feats of the French velocipedists at the Crystal Palace at Easter will believe all the stories of the dashing rides along parapets and the marvellous races that have taken place. The riders frequently wear jockey caps and coloured jackets to distinguish them. One of the most frequent trials of skill is who shall go slowest and who can ride best without any steering apparatus. At these races the prize is often a silver cup or a sum of money. The average length of the course is 1,800 metres, which is nearly equivalent to a mile and a furlong. This distance has been done in four minutes and twenty-five seconds, although a portion of it was over a stone-paved road by a bicycle. A tricycle took two minutes longer to perform the same distance. A racing speed of a mile in five minutes for a distance of two or three miles is very excellent riding.

---

[61] Fops and female clotheshorses

A variety of suggestions have been thrown out with respect to their use. The *Salut de Lyon* states that rural postmen are mounted on them. Telegraph messengers are recommended to use them. Even country doctors and parsons are recommended to try the new iron horse which requires no corn. Artists, electors, and sportsmen are reported as using them. No wonder, then, that when the velocipede was introduced into America, the Yankees exclaimed that 'walking was on its last legs'. They seized with avidity the new idea, though, until the fall of 1868, they do not appear to have excited much popular attention. The *Scientific American* notices their existence in the records of new patents earlier in the year, but gives no description of the new vehicle until later. The other American journals just notice the novelty, and then exclaim that pedestrianism has had its day and must bow before the conquering run of the newer light. Its motion was described as graceful. It was a thing of life, moving with a smooth grace, alike exhilarating and beautiful to behold. They were introduced into the theatres, as in Paris; and the designer in Harper's Weekly represented the New Year, 1869, as coming into the world seated on one of the new contrivances.

The American public were treated to anecdotes of races between velocipedes and the street cars, in which the former were victorious, unless they met with a 'foul' as in the famous race on Indiana Avenue[62], at Chicago. Races took place in Cincinnati, where the prize was a silver cup, worth 100 dollars, for the fastest and another of equal value to the slowest rider. Mr Dana, of the New York Sun, himself an experienced velocipedist, even advocated a project to build an elevated railway from Harlem to the Battery – from one end of New York to the other – for the use of riders of velocipedes only. By this means it was estimated that it would be possible to go from one end of Manhattan Island to the other, barring stoppages and accidents, in an hour. The proposed roadway was to be thirty feet wide, on an iron framework, and the flooring of hard pine. This idea seems to have infected an English inventor, if we may judge from a recent application for a patent.

On the 28th of November, 1868, a public race took place in New York, when the tall French pattern was very generally condemned and the pattern now known as the American (Fig. 5) preferred. It was at first known as the Pickering velocipede and the driving wheel never exceeded three feet in diameter. The most popular pattern was one with the driving-wheel 33 inches high. The frame was made of hydraulic iron tubing, as more simple, lighter, stronger and cheaper than any other

---

[62] Sacramento Daily Union, Volume 36, Number 5569, 1 February 1869: "Recently a gentleman in Chicago, who has been practicing on a velocipede for some time on the sidewalks, came out upon Indiana avenue, and throwing down the gauntlet of defiance dared a street car driver to race with him to Thirty-first street, the terminus of the track. The challenge was accepted by the car driver, although the latter had several lady passengers on board. The race began auspiciously, the horses being driven at a furious pace. The velocipede soon gained upon its competitor, and bade fair to distance it, when an unlucky crack in the sidewalk received the fore wheel, leaving the other, in obedience to the law of its momentum, to turn a sommersault, throwing the rider into the gutter. The car won the race on a "foul."

material. They were made by gauge, so that if any portion met with an accident or wore out, it could be instantly replaced. Of the other three patterns the Monod which was the French pattern (Fig. 3), received a large share of support; and those made by the Brothers Hanlon (Fig. 6) and Messrs Wood were looked upon with favour. At the beginning of the year the demand was so great that there was the greatest difficulty in procuring velocipedes of any pattern. The manufacturers were overwhelmed with orders. The riding-schools and the rooms opened by the manufacturers were found too limited for the accommodation of those anxious to learn the new mode of locomotion. Art galleries were converted into velocipede training institutions; and it was no wonder that the supply fell a month into arrear of the demand.

At the beginning of January it was estimated that there were in New York and its immediate vicinity alone no less than 5,000 persons who either knew how to ride the velocipede or were learning and it was estimated that at least half that number would be mounted during the summer. The side streets were thronged with them; but the city authorities forbade the use of the parks to the 'carriage of the people'. The great difficulty, present and to come, is to find places to ride in.

It was not to be expected that the American carriage manufacturers would permit so profitable a branch of manufacture to slip through their fingers and it was not surprising that they soon began to devote a large portion of their establishments to the manufacture of the popular vehicle. It was understood that any manufacturer was at liberty to make the two-wheeled velocipede in any way he deemed most profitable, no one being aware of the fact that the machine had been duly patented and the exclusive right secured by a little Yankee foresight and ingenuity.

As far back as 1866 the *Scientific American* recorded a patent for the two-wheeled velocipede, with treadles and guiding-arms, known as Lallement's patent; but no one appeared to take notice of the fact, for bicycles were then a thing of the future – a French toy, which no one thought of. When, however, it was obvious that a 'big thing' was to be done in velocipedes. Mr Calvin Witty, of No. 638 Broadway, New York, went quietly to ascertain how the manufacture could be controlled; and he speedily found out the holders of the patent which covered the principle of the bicycle and bought the exclusive right of manufacturing and using treadles and guiding-arms in America. The surprise and indignation of the various manufacturers can be easily judged, when they received a polite intimation from Mr Witty that they were infringing his patent and requesting a settlement for the past infringements. They pooh-poohed the claims, laughed at the notices, held meetings; but they found that the law was on Mr Witty's side and they had to purchase from him a license to manufacture. That gentleman has doubtless hit upon a mine of wealth to reward his shrewdness in forestalling the coming time, unless the opposing claim of Stephen W. Smith, also of New York, is substantiated, for he claims the invention altogether. He states that he invented and perfected the bicycle in New York and afterwards introduced it into France himself by patent. This claim is again disputed by Mr P. W.

Mackenzie, whose 'Cantering Propeller' was patented in 1862 and whose specification embraces all the principles of Lallement's patent (Fig. 1). In the mean time the demand for velocipedes goes on and is yet unsatisfied.

In England we are supposed to be a sensible people, neither affecting the excitement of the French or the sensationalism of the Americans; yet in the matter of velocipedes we have indulged in some strange vagaries. We at least have proposed velocipede railways. We have the 'one-wheeler;' and we, too, have had races. On Wednesday, the 14th of April, 1869, Mr C. A. Booth, the champion of skating, performed the journey from London to Brighton, on a bicycle, 52 miles, in 7½ hours. Previously this had only been done in 9½ hours. In Liverpool the gymnasiums are crowded nightly by expectant riders. Manchester has caught the fever. Birmingham has the symptoms. London is talking over the new excitement. The watering-places are thankful for the new sensation; and embryo riders exclaim –

I shall have no horse to feed,
Though I ride on a velocipede

Ere I say farewell, let me caution velocipedists – past, present and prospective – against expecting too much from any description of velocipede. They do not give power, they only utilize it. There must be an expenditure of power to produce speed. One is inclined to agree with the temperate remarks of Mr Lander, C.E., of Liverpool, rather than with the extravagant enthusiasm of American or French riders. As a means of healthful exercise it is worthy of attention. Certainly not more than forty miles in a day of eight hours can be done with ease: Mr Lander thinks only thirty. If this is correct, it does not beat walking, though velocipedists affirm that double the distance can be done with ease. Much will and must depend on the skill of the rider, the state of the roads and the country to be travelled.

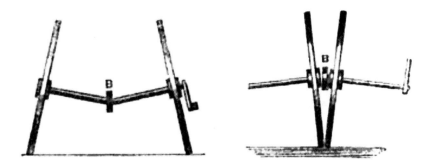

Fig. 30 / 31 – The Elyria Velocipede

(Routledge's Every Boy's Annual, ed. Edmund Routledge, 1870, pp. 284-288, 373-380, 409-416, 472-479, 543-549)

269

ON THE TRAIL OF THE RAMBLER...

It was disappointing that the author of the articles 'Rambles Out Of Margate' had chosen to stay anonymous when his tales first went to print but, in analysing the journals looking for clues as to his identity, two vague hints presented themselves, both in the first instalment:

The first clue was found in the opening paragraph, '...starting from the Head Quarters in Margate...' The second, which supports the first, can be found in paragraph three where our cyclist states: '...to begin my day's ramble, my iron steed is ready having been cleaned and oiled and lamps fixed. I mount and make my way slowly up the High street...' It appears then that our cyclist lived at the bottom end of Margate High Street. With these clues in mind, using local archive material, a quest began in search of our cyclist's identity...

Extensive research led to the following article entitled 'The Margate Cycle Club', in Keble's Gazette dated Saturday 2nd April 1892, printed some six years after our author's Rambles:

> "The first meet and run of the Margate Cycling Club took place last (Thursday) evening, when 35 members took part, including three ladies, and had a most enjoyable run through Westgate to Birchington, and home via Quex Park and Garlinge. The members of the club afterwards assembled at Head-Quarters, Mr Munns's Terrace Hotel, and partook of a substantial meat tea, concluding with a social evening."

Based on the following, it can be deduced that the author of the 'Rambles' was almost certainly the above named gentleman, Samuel Hollands Munns, the owner of the Terrace Hotel:

The rambles had two different starting points: one being somewhere along Margate High Street and the other somewhere along the sea front (Marine Drive). From this, it may be supposed that our author lived in this area of Margate.

The 1881 Census Returns for Margate tell us that not only did Samuel Hollands Munns appear to own property along Marine Drive, (from whence our cyclist started when heading in the Canterbury direction) he also owned property in the bottom part of the High Street – numbers 38, 40 and 42 – from whence our cyclist appears to have started when heading towards Sandwich.

According to the Directory of Kent in 1895, Samuel Hollands Munns owned numbers 14, 15, 16, and 17 Marine Drive, these properties being known as the

Terrace Hotel and the Heart of Oak restaurant – as well as property at Fort Hill and Westgate-on-Sea.

A survey on foot of the places once owned by Mr Munns revealed that numbers 38, 40 and 42 High Street and numbers 14,15, 16 and 17 Marine Drive were interconnected, that is to say, they backed onto each other.

The above information, alongside the evidence of his link to the Margate Cycle Club, points very much in favour of Samuel Hollands Munns being our author. That said, he had two sons who could also be candidates for the title of author: Thomas who was 27 in 1886, or William, who would have been 25 at the time.

In 1881 Thomas was living at 9 Station Road in Westgate as a boot maker and in 1891 he can be found living at 12 Marine Drive, with his wife and two young sons, running a restaurant. As for William, he was living with his father in 1881 but by 1891 was living at 17 High Street, with his wife and young son, as a draper.

In 1886, when this cycling journal was written, Samuel, at the age of 55, appeared to have been a successful businessman. With this in mind it would seem that only Samuel Munns would have been wealthy enough to allow him the freedom to pursue a pastime of rambling around the Kentish countryside.

Our author was obviously a keen cyclist with a passion for nature and his surroundings: his writings were also indicative of him being very conversant in local history. He was a prolific collector of butterflies and moths – a popular pastime for many well-to-do Victorians of this time – for in his rambles he often stops to collect specimens and identifies them by their Latin names, as well as their common names. The local flora are also identified, again, often by their Latin names. He also left behind him some invaluable descriptions of old buildings, their past occupants and characters, some long since gone even at that time.

Biography of Samuel Hollands Munns

Samuel Hollands Munns was born in Margate in 1831. He was the eldest son of shoemaker Stephen Munns and his wife Susannah. Samuel lived with his parents and younger siblings, sisters Susannah and Emma and a brother called Oliver, in Broad Street, Margate. By 1851 the Census Returns show them all living at 9 Duke Street, in Margate's Old Town. Samuel married Mary in June 1855 and had eight children: five boys – Thomas (1858), William (1861), Henry (1869), James (1871), and Charles (1875), and three girls, Charlotte (1865), Clara (1867), and Rose (1873).

By 1858, Samuel with his wife, who was pregnant with their first child, was carrying on business as a boot and shoemaker in Market Street while his father Stephen carried on business as usual at 9 Duke Street. The 1861 Census shows us that Samuel and his young family had moved to 5 Lombard Street. In the 1862 Directory of Kent Samuel was listed as a leather cutter and shoemaker at 144 High Street while his father, who was now 70 years of age, continued as a shoemaker in Market Place. By the time of the 1871 Census Samuel appears to have taken a giant leap and is found living in and owning numbers 38, 40 and 42 High Street. One can only assume that he had inherited his father's property and thus expanded. Later, the 1878 Post Office Directory of Kent shows a Samuel Hollands Munns & Sons, boot & shoe makers, 38 & 40 High Street & Fort Hill, and at the new 'up market' area of Westgate-on-Sea. These businesses would no doubt have provided the funds with which the Terrace Hotel was eventually purchased.

Marine Drive, Margate 1889
Mr Munns's Terrace Hotel is by the coach and horses.

By the 1881 Census Returns we find Samuel Hollands Munns listed as an Alderman and in the 1891 Census as hotel keeper. The 1899 Directory shows Samuel Hollands Munns listed under the heading 'Magistrates for the Borough of Margate', then in 1913 under 'Justices of the Peace for the Borough'. Not bad for one starting life as a boot and shoemaker's son.

Mr Munns apparently ruffled a few feathers during his lifetime, as indicated by the following:

A fine new road for Victorian Margate

A paper prepared for Margate Historical Society by Mick Twyman describes how, from around 1878, the harbour area and the seafront road of Marine Terrace were the subject of a grand road improvement scheme. The finances for the project, and the building of the road, both appear to have been badly mishandled by the Council, costing local ratepayers dear. Mr Munns is described in the article as appearing to be 'a man of fairness and principle', outspokenly questioning the Council's calculations and also casting aspersions on the morality of some of his Council colleagues, who not only seem to have derived considerable personal financial benefit from the scheme, but who also stood accused by Mr Munns of utilising slave labour in the development.

(The Marine Drive Saga, by Mick Twyman, research by Alf Beeching / Margate Historical Society, posted on their website (www.margatehistory.com) on Wed 19th Aug 2009)

"Mr Edgar Pickering and Alderman Fagg were charged at Margate on Wednesday with assaulting Councillor Munns. It appears Mr Pickering considered that his father had been insulted by the complainant, and he accordingly struck him in the street with a cane. Alderman Fagg separated them, and it was alleged that he used unnecessary violence in so doing. Mr Pickering was fined one shilling and costs and the summons against Alderman Fagg was dismissed. Yesterday Mr Samuel Munns was bound over to keep the peace for three months towards Mr Edgar Pickering. After leaving Court on Wednesday the defendant in the present case threatened to assault Mr Pickering."

(Lloyd's Weekly Newspaper (London, England), Sunday, February 22, 1880; Issue 1944)

The Margate Cycle Club made its first appearance in March 1892 and continued for many years, with Samuel as a prominent committee member, hosting the monthly club meetings at 'Headquarters', the Terrace Hotel. It was succeeded by Thanet Road Club in 1947.

Samuel died in 1913 at the age of 82 – his wife soon after, in the same year.

The machine used by our cyclist may well have been one of the new Humber 'Crippers' which had just appeared on the scene in 1885. This tricycle had the then modern pattern of two rear wheels with a front wheel bisecting their track and weighed in at around 75lbs, a far cry from today's super light machines. The evidence for this assertion comes from various remarks made during some of his rambles, such as from Ramble 1: "...The screams proceed from the hare which, in its endeavours to escape from the pursuing dogs, has run straight into one of the big wheels of my machine...". In Ramble 4 he makes fun of "awkward bicyclists". From Ramble 7 "...This road also gradually diminishes to a path across a field of barley. As it is my custom not to turn back unless compelled, I push forward, one wheel of my machine on the path and the other in the barley until I reach a plantation of pine trees, where the path widens sufficiently to allow me to ride comfortably..." This suggests the two large wheels at the back will not both stay on the path.

The 'Cripper'

INDEX

277

OTHER PUBLICATIONS FROM
ŌZARU BOOKS

Reflections in an Oval Mirror
Memories of East Prussia, 1923-45
Anneli Jones

8th May 1945 – VE Day – was Anneliese Wiemer's twenty-second birthday. Although she did not know it then, it marked the end of her flight to the West, and the start of a new life in England.

These illustrated memoirs, based on a diary kept during the Third Reich and letters rediscovered many decades later, depict the momentous changes occurring in Europe against a backcloth of everyday farm life in East Prussia (now the north-western corner of Russia, sandwiched between Lithuania and Poland).

The political developments of the 1930s (including the Hitler Youth, 'Kristallnacht', political education, labour service, war service, and interrogation) are all the more poignant for being told from the viewpoint of a romantic young girl. In lighter moments she also describes student life in Vienna and Prague, and her friendship with Belgian and Soviet prisoners of war. Finally, however, the approach of the Red Army forces her to abandon her home and flee across the frozen countryside, encountering en route a cross-section of society ranging from a 'lady of the manor', worried about her family silver, to some concentration camp inmates.

ISBN: 978-0-9559219-0-2

Travels in Taiwan
Exploring Ilha Formosa
Gary Heath

For many Westerners, Taiwan is either a source of cheap electronics or an ongoing political problem. It is seldom highlighted as a tourist destination, and even those that do visit rarely venture far beyond the well-trod paths of the major cities and resorts.

Yet true to its 16th century Portuguese name, the 'beautiful island' has some of the highest mountains in East Asia, many unique species of flora and fauna, and several distinct indigenous peoples (fourteen at the last count).

On six separate and arduous trips, Gary Heath deliberately headed for the areas neglected by other travel journalists, armed with several notebooks... and a copy of War and Peace for the days when typhoons confined him to his tent. The fascinating land he discovered is revealed here.

ISBN: 978-0-9559219-1-9 (Royal Octavo)
ISBN: 978-0-9559219-8-8 (Half Letter)

Turner's Margate Through Contemporary Eyes
The Viney Letters
Stephen Channing

Margate in the early 19th Century was an exciting town, where smugglers and 'preventive men' fought to outwit each other, while artists such as JMW Turner came to paint the glorious sunsets over the sea. One of the young men growing up in this environment decided to set out for Australia to make his fortune in the Bendigo gold rush.

Half a century later, having become a pillar of the community, he began writing a series of letters and articles for Keble's Gazette, a publication based in his home town. In these, he described Margate with great familiarity (and tremendous powers of recall), while at the same time introducing his English readers to the "latitudinarian democracy" of a new, "young Britain".

Viney's interests covered a huge range of topics, from Thanet folk customs such as Hoodening, through diatribes on the perils of assigning intelligence to dogs, to geological theories including suggestions for the removal of sandbanks off the English coast "in obedience to the sovereign will and intelligence of man".

His writing is clearly that of a well-educated man, albeit with certain Victorian prejudices about the colonies that may make those with modern sensibilities wince a little. Yet above all, it is interesting because of the light it throws on life in a British seaside town some 180 years ago.

This book also contains numerous contemporary illustrations.

ISBN: 978-0-9559219-2-6

Sunflowers
– Le Soleil –
Shimako Murai

A play in one act
Translated from the Japanese by Ben Jones

Hiroshima is synonymous with the first hostile use of an atomic bomb. Many people think of this occurrence as one terrible event in the past, which is studied from history books.

Shimako Murai and other 'Women of Hiroshima' believe otherwise: for them, the bomb had after-effects which affected countless people for decades, effects that were all the more menacing for their unpredictability – and often, invisibility.

This is a tale of two such people: on the surface successful modern women, yet each bearing underneath hidden scars as horrific as the keloids that disfigured Hibakusha on the days following the bomb.

ISBN: 978-0-9559219-3-3

Ichigensan
– The Newcomer –
David Zoppetti

Translated from the Japanese by Takuma Sminkey

Ichigensan is a novel which can be enjoyed on many levels – as a delicate, sensual love story, as a depiction of the refined society in Japan's cultural capital Kyoto, and as an exploration of the themes of alienation and prejudice common to many environments, regardless of the boundaries of time and place.

Unusually, it shows Japan from the eyes of both an outsider and an 'internal' outcast, and even more unusually, it originally achieved this through sensuous prose carefully crafted by a non-native speaker of Japanese. The fact that this best-selling novella then won the Subaru Prize, one of Japan's top literary awards, and was also nominated for the Akutagawa Prize is a testament to its unique narrative power.

The story is by no means chained to Japan, however, and this new translation by Takuma Sminkey will allow readers world-wide to enjoy the multitude of sensations engendered by life and love in an alien culture.

ISBN: 978-0-9559219-4-0

The Margate Tales
Stephen Channing

Chaucer's Canterbury Tales is without doubt one of the best ways of getting a feel for what the people of England in the Middle Ages were like. In the modern world, one might instead try to learn how different people behave and think from television or the internet.

However, to get a feel for what it was like to be in Margate as it gradually changed from a small fishing village into one of Britain's most popular holiday resorts, one needs to investigate contemporary sources such as newspaper reports and journals.

Stephen Channing has saved us this work, by trawling through thousands of such documents to select the most illuminating and entertaining accounts of Thanet in the 18th and early to mid 19th centuries. With content ranging from furious battles in the letters pages, to hilarious pastiches, witty poems and astonishing factual reports, illustrated with over 70 drawings from the time, The Margate Tales brings the society of the time to life, and as with Chaucer, demonstrates how in many areas, surprisingly little has changed.

ISBN: 978-0-9559219-5-7

West of Arabia
A Journey Home
Gary Heath

Faced with the need to travel from Saudi Arabia to the UK, Gary Heath made the unusual decision to take the overland route. His three principles were to stay on the ground, avoid back-tracking, and do minimal sightseeing.

The ever-changing situation in the Middle East meant that the rules had to be bent on occasion, yet as he travelled across Eritrea, Sudan, Egypt, Libya, Tunisia and Morocco, he succeeded in beating his own path around the tourist traps, gaining unique insights into Arabic culture as he went.

Written just a few months before the Arab Spring of 2011, this book reveals many of the underlying tensions that were to explode onto the world stage just shortly afterwards, and has been updated to reflect the recent changes.

ISBN: 978-0-9559219-6-4

Lightning Source UK Ltd.
Milton Keynes UK
UKOW032010070312

188530UK00001B/3/P